# THE MICROWAVE COOKBOOK

*TO SUCCESSFUL
MICROWAVE COOKING
FROM FINDUS*

*AND ANCHOR HOCKING*

⚓ Anchor
Hocking

*MICROWARE*

# THE MICROWAVE COOKBOOK

### Jenny M. Webb

*PUBLISHED BY*
**FORBES PUBLICATIONS**
*IN ASSOCIATION WITH*
**NEW ENGLISH LIBRARY / TIMES MIRROR**

PUBLISHED AUGUST 1978
Reprinted September 1978
Reprinted October 1979
Reprinted September 1980

\*

*Published by*
*New English Library Limited from Barnard's Inn, Holborn, London ECN1 2JR*
*in association with Forbes Publications Limited, Hartree House, Queensway,*
*London W2 4SH*
*Made and printed in Great Britain by Hunt Barnard Printing Ltd., Aylesbury, Bucks.*

0 901 762 282

# Contents

# List of Figures and Tables

**Figures**

**Tables**

# Preface

The microwave oven is still a very new and different appliance for use in the home but it will adapt itself to suit the individual. So I hope that *The Microwave Cookbook* will give you a greater understanding of your microwave oven and that the recipes will form a basis on which to try your own special skills.

It would be remiss of me not to extend my thanks to all those who have encouraged me to write this book but I would especially like to thank Mrs J. Parry-Morris, and also Mrs C. Watson and Mrs G. Hopper, for testing the recipes.

J. M. W.

# Chapter 1

# How a Microwave Oven Works

This is a book for the microwave cook and not just a micro-wave cookbook, since the cook – experienced or otherwise – who wants to buy and enjoy a microwave oven needs to learn a special cooking technique. That way she will get the most out of her appliance and enjoy the speed and variety it suddenly brings to her cuisine. Or should we say 'or *his*' cuisine, since microwave cookery is specially appealing to men of any age? As our cover shows we feel that microwave cooking is a completely unisex job and many wives have told us that their husbands are actually cooking for the family, and not just the party special, since a microwave oven arrived in their home.

You will find that chapters 1–6 are concerned with the basics: what a microwave is and how it cooks food; size of oven (input and output) and features available; microwave terms and definitions; the containers to use; time saving, including cooking tables; and finally maintenance and run-ning costs.

Then from chapter 6 we give you useful general cooking information and tell you how to use the recipe section, ending with 67 pages of specially written recipes for the microwave cook. Every recipe has been tested; the ingredients are easy to buy, and will produce delicious food in a magically short time.

To begin with it is important to remember that although the microwave oven is particularly useful for thawing frozen food and reheating cooked food, it is a real cooking appliance and should be used as such. It will roast, bake, boil, as well as thaw and reheat food, all without any apparent heat, so make the most of its potential and become a real *microwave cook*.

# The Microwave

Microwaves produce many of the benefits we enjoy today. They are electromagnetic waves which make possible infrared radiation, television and radio. In a microwave oven electric power is converted by the magnetron into microwave energy and directed into the oven cavity. As the oven is made of metal, which microwaves cannot penetrate, they are reflected off the walls and base and are absorbed by the food. A wave stirrer or paddle in the top of the oven turns very slowly to distribute the microwaves evenly around the oven.

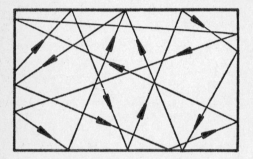

Figure 1. The deflection of microwaves in an oven

All food and liquid is made up of millions of moisture molecules, and these molecules absorb microwaves; each molecule then becomes 'excited' and moves back and forth at a speed of well over two thousand million times a second. This is how heat is generated and therefore food is heated and cooked in a very short time. Wonderful, isn't it?

For a moment let's look at the conventional cooking methods which everyone has been using for years. There are three types of cooking: 1) by *convention*, when heat is transferred from one place to another by movement of the hot material, e.g. baking a cake in a hot oven where heat is transferred through the movement of hot air; 2) by *radiation*, when heat travels through space and is converted back into heat when absorbed, e.g. cooking a piece of steak under a hot grill; 3) by *conduction*, when heat is transferred from a hot to a cold surface which is in contact with it, e.g. frying a cold egg on a hot griddle.

The general principle, when cooking by these conventional methods, is for the heat to penetrate the food fairly slowly, and so, usually, the cooking process cannot be rushed. If you tried to bake a fruit cake at too high a temperature the outside would brown and appear to be cooked, but inside the mixture would be wet and soggy.

Microwaves are essentially of the radiant type of heat, but they are different from the conventional type of radiation cooking because they penetrate more deeply into the food being cooked where they are absorbed and turned into heat. However, microwaves behave differently with different substances: they are either *reflected, transmitted* or *absorbed:*

*Reflected.* Metal is a material which microwaves cannot pass through and so they are reflected off it. So metal material, whatever its form or shape, should not be used as a cooking container, unless a microwave oven manufacturer recommends its use, because the microwaves will not be able to penetrate the container to cook the food.

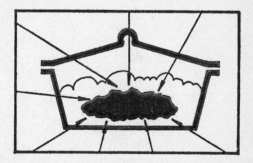

Figure 2. Microwaves being transmitted through a container

*Transmitted.* Microwaves are really rather remarkable when it comes to other sorts of materials such as glass, china, wood and even paper – in general they just pass straight through them. This is because, unlike food, there are few if any moisture molecules to be agitated; consequently all these materials may be used as containers in an oven without them becoming too hot to handle. If they do get too hot it is generally because the food itself has become very hot and is transferring its heat to the container material.

*Absorbed.* At this point it is worth considering the food itself. All food, whether it is meat, fish, dairy products, vegetables or made-up dishes, is formed in basically the same way. Looking at a food it appears to be a solid mass, but if you were

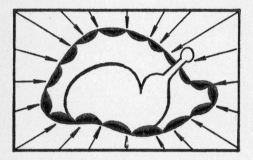

Figure 3. Food absorbing microwaves

able to examine it very closely under a microscope you would find that it is made up of millions of individual moisture molecules. Imagine a long, golden sandy beach. From a distance it will appear to be one solid area of colour, but walk on to the beach, pick up a handful of the sand and you will see that this 'solid' beach is made up of billions of individual grains. So it is with food moisture molecules.

When thawing, heating, or cooking food in a microwave oven the moisture molecules in the food absorb the microwave energy. The waves make each of these molecules twist back and forth at a fantastically high speed and this action in itself creates heat which spreads through the food which, as a result, cooks in minutes rather than hours. Now, you can perhaps appreciate why food *does not brown* – because there is no external heat.

# Chapter 2

## Features of a Microwave Oven
## Microwave Oven Terms Explained
## Running Costs and Care of the Oven

### FEATURES OF A MICROWAVE OVEN

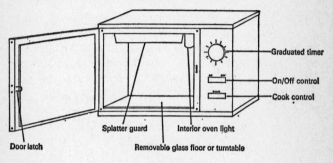

Figure 4.

The basic microwave oven will usually have the following features:

*The Controls.* The simplest controls on a microwave oven could be in the form of a timer and a 'cook' button or switch. Food is simply placed in the oven, the timer set for the cooking time required, and the microwave energy started by switching on the 'cook' control. All microwave ovens automatically switch off when the oven door is opened and not until the door is closed and the 'cook' switch turned on would the microwave energy start again.

The timer could be either clockwork or electric, and it should be remembered that if the oven door is opened the *clockwork* timer will tick on regardless, whereas the electric timer would stop until the cooking operation was restarted.

*Time Control.* Most ovens have at least one timer and the maximum time which can be selected is unlikely to exceed

60 minutes; in general 30-minute timers are fitted. As seconds and minutes are used in microwave cooking it is usual for the minutes at the lower end of the scale to be subdivided in 10–15 second graduations, whereas at the higher end of the scale the graduations increase to 30 seconds, if given at all.

*Cook Control.* Sometimes called the 'start' control, this control is simply a device for switching on the microwave energy, whether you are thawing, heating or cooking.

*On/Off Control.* Apart from its obvious use this switch may also start the cooling fan and bring on the interior oven light. On some ovens there may be a very short delay period of 10 seconds after switching on to allow the power source to warm up prior to use. If there is no 'on/off' control on your oven it will be automatically operated when the oven is connected to the power supply.

*'Off' Indication.* This may indicate that cooking time has finished or may turn off the oven light.

*Interior Oven Light.* This generally lights up as soon as the appliance is switched on. Some models have a separate switch, and one model has the light interlocked with the 'cook' control.

*Splatter Guard.* Sometimes the wavestirrer is protected from any splashes by a protective shield. This is generally removable and should be kept clean according to the manufacturer's instructions (see page 23).

*Removable Glass Floor.* This glass or plastic shelf is housed on the base of the oven floor, and as an integral part of the oven design should always be used as recommended. As it is of a special quality it should *never* be replaced with any other form of glass or plastics if accidentally broken. Its purpose is to act as a spillage plate, to protect the magnetron should the oven be accidentally operated without a food load. Some ovens have a revolving platform or turntable (see page 16).

*Door Latch.* There is considerable variety here and fastening can be either as a door latch on the door itself, a push button on the control panel or incorporated in the door handle, or some ovens may not have a latch at all.

In addition, your microwave oven may have any of these extra features:

*Automatic Defrosting.* As the microwave oven heats food so quickly it is necessary, when thawing frozen foods, to subject the frozen product to the microwave energy in stages, e.g. 30 seconds using microwave energy followed by a short 'rest' period and then repeating the process until the food is evenly thawed. This can be done manually, but on some ovens an automatic defrost control is provided which will automatically pulse the microwave energy so that you can leave it to get on with the job. This may or may not work in conjunction with the timer. (see also page 31.)

*Choice of Microwave Output.* In general once the 'cook' control is operated the microwave energy will remain constant, and the user concentrates simply on time. But a new innovation gives a choice of decreasing the microwave energy by using a dial or slide control, thus introducing a 'slower' cooking rate. Marking may be low, medium and high, or simmer, roast and reheat, or infinitely variable.

*Indicator Lights.* These are a useful benefit to remind the user that a certain operation has been set, is in process or finished.

*Audible Reminders.* These may be in the form of a bell or buzzer to remind you that the 'cook' process is completed.

*Cooking Guide.* A panel on the front of the oven giving the basic information needed for various cooking operations.

*Cooking Container Kits.* These kits, specially designed for the particular microwave oven, are an optional extra from some manufacturers. The range of dishes is extensive and it is sometimes possible to obtain a special roasting dish complete with trivet which may be used to support the meat or poultry.

*Meat and Food Thermometers.* These may only be used if the manufacturer specifically states that it is possible, and instructions must be strictly observed. Some manufacturers supply a thermometer specially designed for their oven. The thermometer will have a pointed probe to insert in the meat or food and a temperature dial at the top. It is not possible to read the thermometer through an oven door, so the door must be opened periodically to check the reading.

*Revolving Platform.* During normal cooking or heating of food in a microwave oven it is necessary to either stir the food or turn the dish within the oven to obtain even heating of the food. At least two manufacturers produce an oven with a revolving platform, and this automatically turns throughout the heating and cooking process.

*Portable Trolley.* A sturdy trolley on wheels can be obtained as an optional extra which enables you to move your oven easily from room to room.

*Browning Element.* A built-in browning element is not a common feature on microwave ovens but when fitted it enables the cook to brown foods by the use of a conventional element housed at the top of the oven.

*Browning Dish.* As a basic microwave oven is not capable of browning foods this is a special dish designed to overcome this problem. It is made of a glass ceramic material, supported on small feet, and has a special coating on the bottom which is heated by the microwaves to a higher temperature than the food would normally be. The empty browning dish is pre-heated for different times, depending on the food to be browned. Food is then placed on the dish and its surface is seared and browned. During the cooking period the food is reversed to brown the other side. As these browning dishes can get very, very hot they should be handled with care. Do not place on a work surface without protection underneath. Sometimes a detachable handle is supplied. Take care when cleaning not to damage the coating; use only a plastics scouring pad and only apply to the topside of the dish. (See also page 32.)

*Thawing Plate and Cover.* One manufacturer produces a mat and cover designed to reduce the likelihood of dehydration around the edges of frozen products during the thawing

16

process. The round ceramic mat has a metal cover similar to a plate cover. The cover has a plastic handle and the underside accommodates a ceramic dish enclosed in plastics, and the microwaves are only able to pass through these areas. The ceramic retains heat and so contributes to the thawing process.

*Keep Warm/Stay Hot Control.* This control enables food and dishes to be kept warm without continuing the cooking process.

*Touch Control.* The controls are built into the panel giving a smooth easy-to-clean area and instead of buttons, knobs or dials it is only a question of touching the appropriate section on the control panel.

*Slo-Cook.* A control which enables the output to be lowered by either reducing the microwave output or by 'pulsing', thus slowing down the cooking time.

*Stacking Plate Rings.* Made of TPX and self-explanatory in so much as they can be used for stacking plates of food in either a freezer or a microwave oven.

*Two Power-Level Cooking.* The basic oven size remains the same but the microwaves enter the oven from the sides rather than the top. Thus, by clever design, two cooking levels may be employed simultaneously. However, this revolutionary design has only recently been introduced in the USA and is unlikely to be available in the UK for some time.

## Microwave Leakage

All ovens have special safety devices which switch off the microwave energy when the oven door is opened. However, when the door is closed it may be possible that a minute leakage is present. In accordance with the safety standards the leakage may not exceed more than 5 mW/cm² measured at the distance of 2 inches from any part of the oven during its life. Certainly, in the new condition the leakage is virtually nothing and it should be remembered that any leakage would decrease very rapidly as the distance from the source increases.

Microwaves are similar to radio waves and visible light waves and should not be confused with such rays as gamma

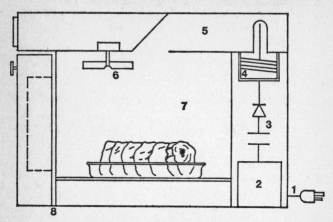

Figure 5. A basic microwave oven

1. *The flexible cord* – The appliance is switched on and the electricity flows to the

2. *Power Transformer* – which increases the 240 alternating voltage to a very high alternating voltage. This passes into

3. *A high voltage rectifier and capacitor* – which changes the high alternating voltage into unidirectional, i.e. direct voltage. This unidirectional voltage is applied to

4. *The magnetron* – which converts this direct voltage to a very high frequency alternating voltage and so generates microwave energy. This energy is then conducted via

5. *The waveguide* – which directs it towards the oven cavity. As the microwaves enter the oven

6. *The wave stirrer (paddle)* – turns very slowly to distribute the microwaves evenly around the oven.

7. *The oven cavity* – being constructed of metal safely contains the microwaves which are deflected off the walls and base to be absorbed by the food.

8. *The oven door* – and the surrounding frame are provided with special seals constructed to ensure that the microwaves are confined within the cavity. In addition it is so arranged that as the door is opened the microwave power is automatically shut off.

rays and X-rays which are of the ionising type. To quote Professor James Van Allan of the University of Iowa: 'My judgement of microwave oven hazard is about the same as the likelihood of getting a skin tan from moonlight.'

## The Magnetron

Many people think of the magnetron as the heart of the microwave oven, as it is this component which transforms the electrical energy into electromagnetic energy generally known as microwaves. Of course, there are other important parts in the oven but this is the one which is normally mentioned and the guarantee given for the magnetron may be longer than the usual time of one year.

## Security in Design

All reputable microwave oven manufacturers ensure that their appliance is electrically safe and that the microwave leakage is insignificant. However, a further guarantee of safety is the BEAB Approval label for household appliances, or the Electricity Council label for commercial catering equipment.

These labels confirm that the appliance meets safety requirements and operates within the microwave leakage limits set out in the appropriate British Standard Specification. These are: for domestic ovens, BS 3456: Specification for Household Electrical Appliances: Part 2: Section 2.33: 1976 Microwave Ovens; and for the commercial catering microwave ovens, BS 5175: 1976 The Specification for the Safety of Commercial Electrical Appliances Using Microwave Energy for Heating Foodstuffs.

## Siting Your Microwave Oven

Now that you begin to appreciate the design and performance of a microwave oven it is interesting to know how versatile its siting may be. In general the oven will not require any installation other than a suitable plug, i.e. a 13 or 15 amp three-pin plug. It is not a very heavy piece of equipment and can be used almost anywhere.

For instance, in the kitchen it can be used on a table or unit top, or as part of a built-in scheme. As it creates no cooking smells or heat it can easily be used in the dining-room, either on a sideboard or on a trolley; it is ideal for use in a bed-sitter, where space is often at a premium; and finally it is very suitable in a sickroom, where meals and hot drinks may be needed at 'unsocial' hours and with the minimum of fuss.

## MICROWAVE TERMS EXPLAINED

### The Wattage (Input and Output)

Most people are familiar with the term 'wattage' which is the unit of electrical power supplied. To enable the householder to use electrical power it has to be converted to a useful form such as heat, light and motive power.

In general, many people assume that the output will be the same as the input regardless of the work it is designed to do, but this is not always so. For instance, a 1000 watt heater when connected to the electricity supply will give the user 1000 watts of heat. On the other hand, a 100 watt light bulb when fitted into a lamp holder does give light but not 100 watts of it as some of the energy is in the form of heat. This can be experienced by holding a hand near a light bulb when it is on.

Similarly, a 500 watt motor on a vacuum cleaner when connected to the electricity supply will give sufficient suction to pick up dust, but not 500 watts as some of the energy is in the form of heat. This is why the air is warm when it is expelled from the non-suction end of a cleaner.

Therefore, the wattage stated on the appliance is the total energy input, not all of which is functionally used.

As with all electrical appliances, the microwave oven has a stated input (wattage) but confusion can occur because the manufacturer is likely to quote a figure for both input and output. These will not agree. For instance, the input for a microwave oven could be given as 1000 watts whereas the output may be stated as 500 watts. This is because some of the watts have been used to convert the electrical energy into microwaves. Thus, '500 watts' indicates the actual microwave energy available for thawing, heating, and cooking.


### Equalising Time or Standing Time

An expression used to indicate that the heat which has been created in the food is given the opportunity to spread to other parts of the food. This is usual when thawing. (See page 31.)


### Carry-Over Cooking or Standing

After the cooked food has been removed from the oven the heat created within the food during the process can continue to cook the food and this can sometimes be used as part of the cooking operation. (See page 31.)

*Note:* Should either standing time or carry-over cooking be necessary the recipe will say so.


## RUNNING COSTS

The running costs of the microwave oven can be very low as all the microwave energy is concentrated into the food being thawed, heated or cooked. As there is no need to preheat the

Table 1. Energy consumption in microwave cooking compared to conventional cooking

| Fresh Product | Method of Cooking | kWh |
|---|---|---|
| 4 Chicken pieces | Microwave<br>Conventional oven | 0·402<br>1·139 |
| Topside of beef | Microwave<br>Conventional oven | 0·411<br>1·723 |
| Wholemeal bread | Microwave<br>Conventional oven | 0·097<br>0·914 |
| Apple suet pudding | Microwave<br>Hotplate | 0·226<br>0·633 |
| Pineapple upside down cake | Microwave<br>Conventional hotplate/oven | 0·147<br>1·018 |
| 2 Herrings | Microwave<br>Grill | 0·037<br>0·213 |

*Scource: Electricity Council Appliance Testing Laboratories*

Table 2. Energy consumption in microwave cooking compared to conventional cooking: vegetables

| Fresh Product | Method of Cooking | kWh |
|---|---|---|
| Brussel Sprouts | Microwave<br>Hotplate | 0·10<br>0·20 |
| Mushrooms | Microwave<br>Hotplate | 0·08<br>0·18 |
| Boiled potatoes | Microwave<br>Hotplate | 0·28<br>0·26 |
| Boiled parsnips | Microwave<br>Hotplate | 0·27<br>0·30 |
| White cabbage | Microwave<br>Hotplate | 0·24<br>0·24 |
| Leeks | Microwave<br>Hotplate | 0·27<br>0·24 |
| Sweet peppers | Microwave<br>Hotplate | 0·09<br>0·26 |
| Cauliflower flourets | Microwave<br>Hotplate | 0·27<br>0·20 |

*Source: Electricity Council Appliance Testing Laboratories*

oven there is very little, if any, loss of heat. Therefore, the running costs tend to be less than for conventional cooking appliances.

But it would be misleading to say that the microwave oven will always prove to be an energy-saving appliance as much depends on the quantities of food cooked and the type of operation employed. Tables 1 and 2 illustrate this point. Although the use of a microwave oven will tend to reduce energy consumption it should be noted that when the oven is used to carry out such operations as the thawing of food, energy will be used where previously food would have been thawed at room temperature. To be balanced against this are speed of operation, convenience, comfort, labour saving.

## CARE OF THE OVEN

The microwave oven must be one of the few cooking appliances which require so little effort to keep clean. All that is needed is a quick wipe over with a damp cloth after use. Abrasives and other proprietary cleaners must never be used unless specially recommended by the oven manufacturer.

The interior of the oven door is cleaned in exactly the same way but under no circumstances should a knife or any other implement be used, especially in the area of the door seal. If there is an air filter or splatter guard fitted, the manufacturer's instruction booklet will give the appropriate cleaning instructions. (See page 14.)

Clean the exterior with a soft damp cloth and never allow water to enter into the exterior vents.

Should the oven smell after cooking a strong-smelling food, this can be removed by boiling some water and lemon juice in the oven for a few minutes.

**Important**

★ Always keep the oven clean, particularly around the door seal.

★ Never lean on the oven door, use it for resting on, or for drying teatowels.

★ If a fault occurs do not use the oven and always obtain the help of a qualified service engineer.

★ Never dismantle the oven and always disconnect the power supply before carrying out a major cleaning operation.

# Chapter 3

## Containers and Utensils
## Covering and Wrapping Foods
## The Shape of Container to Use

### CONTAINERS AND UTENSILS

The following list of containers and materials suitable for use in a microwave oven is given as a guide from which to choose. However, once again it is always advisable to read the microwave oven manufacturer's instruction book, and if there is any doubt as to the suitability of any particular container, the supplier of either the oven or container should be consulted. Particular care should be taken when reading the instruction book as if it has been issued by a foreign manufacturer the definitions may be different to those found in this country.

The best container to use is one which is non-porous, allows the microwaves to be transmitted into food, and will not melt or warp.

### Containers and Materials Suitable for Use in a Microwave Oven

| | |
|---|---|
| Paper ... ... ... | ... Food support or covering |
| Greaseproof Paper ... | ... Wrapping or covering |
| Cotton or Linen Napkins | ... Wrapping or food support |
| Straw ... ... ... | ... Food support |
| Wood ... ... ... | ... Food support |
| Table Glass ... ... | ... Short-term heating |
| China ... ... ... | ... Most operations |
| Oven to Table Glass ... | ... Most operations |
| Glass Ceramic ... | ... Most operations |
| Plastics Cling-Type Film | ... Covering or wrapping |
| Boil-in-the-Bag Pouches | ... Heating or cooking |

| Roasting Bags | ... | ... | Cooking |
| Pottery | ... | ... | ... | Most operations |
| Some Plastics | ... | ... | Heating |
| Special Microwave Containers | | As manufacturer directs |

## Containers and Materials not Suitable for Use in a Microwave Oven

Glued-on Handles
Metal
Metal Decorations
Metal Glaze
Metal Ingredients
Some Plastics
Plastics Storage Bags
Lead Crystal or Antique Glass or China
Waxed Paper

## Not Sure

Foil ... ... ... Follow the manufacturer's advice

In some instances it may be difficult to know if a container is suitable for use. For example, if porous containers include metal in their ingredients, they will deflect the microwaves and affect the cooking results. In which case a simple test can be made:

*Test for Oven-to-Table Ware, China, Pottery, Ceramic Cookware*

1) Place a cup of water in or on the container being tested.
2) Put them into the oven and set the timer for $1\frac{1}{2}$ minutes.
3) Remove the cup of water and the container.

*Check*

1) If the water is hot and the container cool, it is suitable for use.
2) If the water is luke warm and the container is warm

26

around the edges, it is only suitable for short period heating of food.

3) If the water is cool and the container is very warm or hot, it is not suitable for use.

*Test for Glass and Plastic Containers*
1) Place a cup of water in or on the container being tested.
2) Put them into the oven and set the timer for 10–15 seconds.
3) Remove the cup of water and the container.

*Check*
If the glass or plastics feel warm, it is not suitable for use.

**Special Microwave Containers**

Both microwave oven and independent manufacturers are now in the position of supplying special microwave containers in various shapes and materials. Lakeland Plastics for example include containers which can be used for a variety of foods but have the added advantage of also being suitable for use in the freezer. Thus, freezer to microwave oven or vice versa can be an added advantage.

**General Caution**

★ If the oven has a browning element or if auxiliary radiant heat is used, then do not use any container which is inflammable.

★ If the manufacturer allows foil to be used for protecting small areas of food, such as the tail of a fish, do not allow it to touch any part of the oven interior.

★ Always pierce bags, pouches and wrappings to ensure that any steam can escape.

# COVERING AND WRAPPING FOOD

★ If you want to keep the food moist then cover or wrap it, e.g. fish or a casserole.

★ Foods which are intended to be dry, such as breads, pastries and cakes, do not usually need to be covered or wrapped.

★ Foods which may splatter can be covered with a piece of greaseproof paper or kitchen paper.

★ When reheating bread, cakes, etc., stand them on a piece of absorbent paper to avoid the underneath becoming soggy.

# THE SHAPE OF CONTAINER TO USE

★ The more regular the shape the better. For example, a round shape is better than an oval shape, as quicker cooking might occur at the 'points' of the oval and a less evenly cooked product might result.

★ A straight-sided container is better than a curved one such as a bowl, as the microwaves can penetrate more evenly.

★ A large, shallow dish is better than a smaller, deeper one, as the food is not so thick and offers greater exposure area to the microwaves. (See also page 37.)

★ When thawing, choose a dish which will keep the thawed contents fairly close together. In a large dish the melted liquid will spread out and start to heat and cook before the rest of the food has had time to thaw.

# Chapter 4

## Using Your Microwave Oven
## How to Ensure Even Cooking
## Thawing Food
## Browning Food

## USING YOUR MICROWAVE OVEN

What does a cook have to consider and calculate when preparing any foods to be cooked by conventional methods? She will need to consider some if not all of the following points:

1) What is the menu? How is it to be prepared?
2) What type of cooking is needed? Is it to be by conduction, radiation, convection or all three?
3) Would the oven or grill have to be preheated? Is boiling water needed?
4) What temperatures are to be used? How long has each food to be cooked?
5) At what time should each cooking operation start to ensure that all of it will be ready at the same time?

It is at this point that the benefits of a microwave oven can be appreciated. It does not detract from the art of cooking, but will allow the user to produce foods both quickly and efficiently without having to make too many complicated calculations.

Using the microwave oven is very easy and it is not necessary to be aware of all the things which can affect the heating and cooking results. Generally it is just a case of following the manufacturer's cookery book (or this one) and excellent results can be obtained every time.

Certainly, the microwave oven simplifies the art of cooking as, in general, it is only a question of thinking of time in relation to the quantity of food being prepared. Nevertheless, it is sometimes nice to know what also can contribute to the type of result obtained and the following list may be of interest:

*Initial temperature of the food.* Cold food from a refrigerator will take longer to cook, whereas food at room temperature will cook more quickly.

*Thickness and shape of the food.* The thick parts will take longer to cook than the thin section, e.g. a leg of lamb, but a regular shape such as a piece of rolled lamb will cook more evenly.

*Volume of food.* One jacket potato will take about $3\frac{1}{2}$–4 minutes to cook, but two jacket potatoes will take about $6\frac{1}{2}$–7 minutes.

*Density of the food.* Porous food such as bread will cook more quickly, but dense and heavy foods such as a chop take longer.

*Moisture content.* The more moisture or water in the food the more energy is needed to heat it.

## HOW TO ENSURE EVEN COOKING

Figure 6. Illustration showing dish rotation

Although the greatest penetration of microwaves is at the first 35–50 mm ($1\frac{1}{2}$–2 in), there is sufficient heat generated in the food to thaw, heat, or cook almost anything from a thin piece of bacon to a family size joint. However, to avoid uneven cooking it is simply a case of turning over or stirring the food, or rotating the dish. How often you need to do this will depend upon the type and quantity of food being cooked but when thawing, heating, or cooking small quantities it is usually not necessary to turn over or stir the food, as the microwaves will penetrate to the centre.

Some of the newer microwave cookers have a revolving turntable which virtually eliminates the need to turn food manually.

**Standing Time or Carry-Over Cooking**

As microwaves thaw, heat and cook in a different way to conventional cooking, the heating effect can continue for a short period after the food has been removed from the oven. Thus, with larger items such as joints of meat, by removing the food from the oven and allowing it to stand for some minutes an evenly cooked, acceptable result is achieved. Because of this continued cooking it is wiser to undercook, remembering that undercooked food can always be returned to the oven but overcooked food hasn't a second chance. (See also page 21.)

## THAWING FOOD

Food, when frozen, forms lots of ice crystals all of which are of different sizes and when the food is thawed in the conventional way the smallest crystals melt first, then gradually the larger ones start to melt. The process is exactly the same in a microwave oven but much faster. However, because the microwaves can also cook food it is possible to obtain a result where the food is partly thawed, partly cooked and even icy in some areas. To avoid this, many ovens incorporate an automatic defrosting control. This automatically switches the microwaves on and off, which means that during the off period the larger ice crystals have the opportunity to melt. (See also page 21.)

The result is an evenly thawed product ready for cooking

or eating. With smaller pieces of food it is not usually necessary to thaw in this way. If the oven does not have an automatic defrost facility then it may be necessary for the user to switch the oven on and off manually.

**Note:**

★ It is most important to thaw foods, such as large joints of meat or poultry, before cooking. In these instances, it is usually recommended to leave the thawed food to stand for about 15–20 minutes before actually starting to cook it.

★ When thawing liquids, it is possible to speed up the operation by breaking the food up with a fork during the thawing operation, and stirring the contents occasionally.

★ When thawing certain foods, such as broccoli or cauliflower florets, there may be some pieces of ice, and it is worth removing these during the thawing process as this will speed up the operation.

★ When thawing fruit it is better to only partially thaw in the microwave oven, remove and leave it to stand to finish thawing, otherwise the fruit could start to cook.

BROWNING FOOD

Food should appeal to the eye and although the microwave oven can do most things the microwaves by themselves cannot brown food. In general this non-browning may not affect many of the foods we eat but with foods such as meat a browning effect is likely to be desirable. This is simple to achieve by using either the grill or frying pan to brown the outside of the food and then using the microwave oven to do the speedy cooking. However, there is another way: a special dish designed primarily for browning foods in the microwave oven. This dish is only intended for use in a microwave oven and is not suitable for use in or on the top of conventional heating units.

By using a browning dish, the range of cooking in the oven can be increased to include such items as pancakes, fried eggs, toasted sandwiches, crispy bacon, and steaks. The shape of the dish can vary but, in general, it is made of a glass ceramic material with a special coating on the base which is heated by the microwaves to a higher temperature than the food would normally achieve.

The empty browning dish is preheated for different times depending upon the food to be cooked. Once preheated, the food is placed on the dish and the surface of the food is seared and browned. During the cooking period the food is turned over so that it browns on the other side.

Unlike most dishes used in the microwave oven some browning dishes can get very, very hot; therefore, they should be handled with care. If the dish is placed on a work surface during or after use it is advisable to put a protective tray underneath. (See also page 16.)

## So What Makes the Microwave Oven so Special?

Simply its versatility:

★ It can roast, poach, steam, boil, bake, thaw, heat, and even soften ingredients such as butter, and melt chocolate.

★ It is economical because the energy produced is directed into the food, it is not wasted elsewhere, for example, through oven walls. So in general, the overall fuel consumption is reduced as is the time spent working in the kitchen.

★ It is fast because thawed, heated, or cooked food can be produced in a fraction of the time that would normally be taken when using conventional methods of cooking.

★ It is easy to use as usually there are only two controls and a timer, and learning how to operate them is simple.

There are many other advantages, such as:

★ Being able to cook food in the container in which it is going to be served.

★ The kitchen will remain cooler because no oven preheating is needed; and as the microwave oven cooks so quickly, there is very little heat loss through the oven walls.

★ Cooking smells are reduced because the speed of the cooking is so fast and the cooking operation is carried out in the confined area of the oven.

★ The oven interior does not get too hot so it is not possible for foods to 'burn on'; thus oven cleaning is almost a thing of the past.

★ The hazard of handling hot dishes is virtually non-existent as it is the food which gets hot, not the containers and oven.

★ Because of the design of the microwave oven and its method of heating and cooking, decorating the kitchen becomes a less frequent chore.

★ Because foods such as vegetables are being cooked quickly and with very little water more nutrients are retained, and because the microwave oven can reheat food at high speed there is less chance of losing other nutrients which previously would have been lost through steaming or boiling.

It would seem, then, that the microwave oven is designed to replace the conventional cooker, but this is not the idea. It is, of course, invaluable where there are no other means of cooking, such as in a bed-sitting-room, but for the average user it will best be used in conjunction with other appliances. It is important not to feel guilty because you continue to use conventional appliances, and certainly for the first month or so you may not use your microwave oven to the full. Most people who buy a microwave oven will have been cooking for many years and so tend to fall back on their well tried, traditional way of working. But as you grow to understand and appreciate your microwave oven you will use it *in preference* to the conventional methods, because microwave cooking techniques will make many of the old working methods obsolete.

# Chapter 5

## Tips for the Microwave Oven User

A microwave oven is very versatile and the following list gives some examples of what a boon it is. However, each oven may not necessarily be able to complete every operation listed, e.g. drying flowers. So check your manufacturer's instruction book for further information.

### Some Examples of What a Microwave Oven Will Do

| | |
|---|---|
| Melt ... ... ... | Butter, chocolate, jellies, cheese |
| Boil ... ... ... | Water, drinks, soups |
| Soften ... ... | Butter, icings, frostings |
| Roast ... ... | Poultry, game, meat |
| Warm ... ... | Babies bottles and lotions |
| Sauté... ... ... | Meat, vegetables |
| Casserole ... ... | Fish and meat dishes |
| Bake ... ... | Some pastries, cakes, yeast mixtures |
| Dry ... ... ... | Bread, flowers |
| Steam ... ... | Suet dishes, fish |
| Poach ... ... | Fish, eggs |
| Heat/Cook ... ... | Cold dishes |
| Reheat/Thaw ... | Frozen foods |
| Toast ... ... | Nuts, desiccated coconut |

### But ...

It cannot reheat battered foods successfully, undertake deep fat frying, or brown certain foods, such as meat, without the aid of a browning plate, or conventional grill or oven.

## Important

★ First, do get to know your oven by carefully reading and following the manufacturer's instructions.

★ Never use metal in any form, unless the manufacturer states this is in order.

★ When a dish requires stirring during cooking time, this can be done in the oven as the oven is automatically switched off when the door is opened.

★ Never attempt to boil an egg, unless the manufacturer gives specific instructions, as the pressure which builds up in the egg during the fast cooking time may cause it to shatter. This creates a cleaning problem and may damage the oven.

★ Always prick or cut the skins of tomatoes, potatoes, whole fruit etc., to allow the steam to escape.

★ Some ovens should never be switched on without anything in them, so leave a glass of water inside just in case someone switches it on by accident.

★ Always use unsalted butter for brushing foods as the salt in butter can absorb moisture and toughen the food.

★ Never sprinkle food with salt. Season it afterwards.

★ Use a container large enough to avoid the 'boiling over' of milk, or milk-based sauces, soups, etc.

★ Allow extra cooking time for stuffed meat and poultry.

★ Tough meat cannot be tenderised by cooking with microwaves. Therefore, cook the tougher cuts in the conventional manner by braising, stewing or casseroling, but use the oven to thaw or reheat.

★ Cook joints and poultry in a roasting bag.

★ If cooking more than one type of food at a time be sure to remove the food which is cooked first, so that it does not overcook while the other food finishes cooking.

★ To brown meat and poultry use the grill, frypan or browning dish to obtain the desired colour.

★ When thawing foods, the operation can be speeded up if the half-thawed food is gently broken up with a fork, and any large pieces of ice removed from the container.

★ Containers do remain relatively cool especially if compared with those employed for conventional cooking, but remember they can get fairly hot as a result of high temperatures reached by the food. Coverings should be removed with care to avoid suddenly releasing trapped steam.

★ To save the chore of washing up dishes make full use of non-metallic tableware by getting into the habit of cooking and serving in it.

★ Foods cook more evenly, if they are of an even depth. Therefore, with foods that can be arranged in this way, e.g. vegetables of the same size and depth, casseroles, chops, etc., it is better to spread them evenly over a larger container, rather than piled into a smaller one. (See also page 28.)

★ Food is very, very hot when it is removed from the oven, therefore, if checking for seasoning, allow the food to cool in a spoon before tasting it.

★ Coffee or chocolate powder and sugar can be added to cold milk or water before heating. But if this causes the drink to 'froth' during the heating period it is better to add the sugar and powder after heating.

★ To thaw tinned drinks – place the tin in hot water for a minute or two; remove the lid at both ends and push the frozen drink into a container to thaw in the oven.

★ Most food can be successfully reheated but in some instances the result may be unacceptable; for example, fried chipped potatoes or foods which have been cooked in batter. The food is piping hot, but due to the moisture created during heating the crisp exterior becomes limp.

★ Although small amounts of butter, etc., may be melted in the microwave oven, shallow or deep fat frying must not be attempted.

★ Foil, used in small quantities is useful to 'shield' the food, such as the tail of a fish, but must only be used if recommended by the manufacturer. (See pages 26, 27.)

★ If more than 0.56 litres (1 pint) of boiling water is required, use an electric kettle as it is quicker and cheaper.

★ Unlike conventional oven cooking, the microwave oven door can be opened as often as needed without spoiling the food. The oven switches off automatically when the door is opened.

★ Soufflés and egg custards may be cooked in some ovens, where the microwave energy can be reduced. However, if this facility is not available, success can sometimes be achieved if the container holding the mixture is placed in a further dish containing water.

★ Instruction and recipe books are supplied by the microwave oven manufacturers but if using other microwave cookbooks (such as this one) remember that features and energy outputs may differ from oven to oven, so procedures and cooking times may need adjusting.

★ Use the minimum amount of water when cooking most fresh vegetables.

★ Never grease and flour a container – grease only or line the utensil with cling-type film.

★ When cooking eggs prick the yolks with a wooden cocktail stick to prevent them losing their domed shape.

★ Avoid using plastics containers if the food has a high fat or sugar content, as a higher temperature is reached compared to other liquids and ingredients.

★ The less depth of food the quicker it will heat or cook, as the microwaves can penetrate more quickly.

★ Deep fat frying should not be attempted, but it is possible to sauté vegetables or fry an egg.

★ Meat and poultry sometimes make a popping noise during cooking but this is normal.

# Chapter 6

# General Cooking Information

### Looking at Individual Foods

The average output of the domestic microwave oven is in the region of 600 watts and the cooking times suggested throughout this chapter are based on this output. But it is important to note that the times and methods given are only intended as a guide and that reference should always be made to the manufacturer's instruction and recipe book.

When using these recipes with a 700 watt microwave cooker, cooking times should be reduced slightly.

### Bread

Many types of bread can be baked in a microwave oven, but the bread will not be browned or have a crisp crust. If, however, a soft crust is acceptable and a brown flour is being used the microwave oven will produce a very palatable loaf. If a browned crust is required, use the microwave oven in conjunction with a conventional oven to speed up the cooking process. Firstly, cook the bread in the microwave oven and then transfer it to a very hot preheated conventional oven to crisp and brown. For example, to bake a 500 g (1 lb) loaf, cook it in the microwave oven for about 3 minutes and then transfer it to the conventional oven for about 8 minutes.

The non-metallic container used for bread-making needs to be greased, or lined with greaseproof paper, or cling film. The cooking operation should be carried out uncovered. It is not advisable to flour the container as this will create a cooked flour film on the bread.

Frozen breads can be speedily thawed. A bread roll takes about 15–20 seconds, but if more than one roll or piece of bread is being thawed, then the time would be increased. For example, one slice of bread would take about 15 seconds to thaw, two slices 25 seconds, three slices 35 seconds. Bread rolls take a slightly shorter period. It is advisable, as with most thawing operations, to rest the produce for a minute or two before serving. To thaw bread place it on a piece of absorbent paper or towel and don't cover.

Frozen bread dough can be thawed and proved in a microwave oven. The complete operation would take about 1 hour for a 500 g (1 lb) loaf. In this instance, the method used is to subject the dough to bursts of microwave energy of approximately 3 minutes and then allow a 3 minute rest period. This operation should be continued until the dough has doubled in size, and could take twelve or more operations.

A microwave oven is not able to toast bread. If, however, bread is toasted in the conventional manner, it can be used as a base for toppings which may be heated or cooked afterwards in the microwave oven. For example, melted cheese on toast would take about 15–20 seconds.

The oven is also capable of dehydrating bread so if rusks are needed they can be obtained in a very few minutes. It is important to remember that bread dehydrates if heated for too long, and the end result is a tough, rubbery product. So when bread is being cooked or reheated it is advisable to undercook or heat, and to remember that the centre of the product will invariably be hotter than the outside.

## Beverages

Always use a cup or mug large enough to avoid the drink boiling over. Remember cold drinks can be reheated and frozen drinks can be quickly thawed. To speed up the thawing operation break the liquid up with a fork and stir occasionally.

The time taken to heat any liquid will depend upon its initial temperature and the size of cup or mug. As a guide, one cup of water would take $1-1\frac{1}{2}$ minutes, two cups $2-2\frac{1}{2}$ minutes, three cups $3\frac{1}{2}-4$ minutes.

## Bottling

Make the bottling syrup in the oven, use small jars, add the fruit and cook this in the jars. Do not use metal tops in the oven and be extra careful when handling the jars as they will be very hot.

## Biscuits

Biscuit mixtures which are cut after cooking are usually better than individually cooked biscuits. Use a flat greased, non-metallic plate or greaseproof paper. Do not flour the plate as this will form a crust on the mixture. A covering is not usually required.

Thaw frozen biscuits on a piece of absorbent paper. One biscuit would take approximately 15 seconds to thaw but the time needs to be increased if a number are to be thawed at any one time.

## Blanching for the Freezer

It is possible to carry out blanching in the microwave oven. The preparation of the vegetables both before and after blanching remains the same but the quantity of water used is very much less, only about 75 ml (3 fl oz) to 500 g (1 lb) of vegetables. The vegetables and water are placed in a large covered container and cooked for approximately 4–6 minutes but it is important (a) to stir or turn the food once during the operation, (b) give a standing time of 1 minute before cooling in ice water, (c) not to overcook as the vegetables would be less sweet and more starchy, (d) to blanch small quantities at a time.

## Cake-Making

It is possible to use conventional recipes but these may need adjusting as sometimes with microwave cooking the taste of the raising agent is more noticeable. If this be the case, it is worth reducing the raising agent by up to 25%. Slacker mixtures seem to be the most successful and standing about five minutes before cooking can often improve the height of rise.

On the whole cakes which contain a high proportion of dried fruit do not cook well.

Any non-metallic container may be used, including paper and even ice cream cones. If a solid container is used it may be greased or lined with greaseproof paper or cling-type film. Do not flour the container as this will result in a crust forming on the cooked product. Cakes rise very well in a microwave oven, so the containers should not be more than half filled with the uncooked mixture.

Cakes may start to rise unevenly and should this happen just turn the container. In some instances, the container should be given a quarter turn about every $1\frac{1}{2}$–2 minutes, when the total cooking time is in the region of 6 minutes. Small fairy cakes take a very much shorter cooking time. For example, one small cake will take 15–20 seconds, two will take 30–40 seconds, six will take $1\frac{1}{2}$–2 minutes, and twelve will take 3–4 minutes. Check whether or not a cake is cooked by inserting a cocktail stick or skewer when the cake is removed from the oven. If the stick or skewer is clean, the cake is cooked. It is better to underbake rather than overbake your cake, as it will continue to cook when removed from the oven. Once the cake is removed from the oven it should be left in the container for about 10 minutes before turning out.

### Thawing

A microwave oven is able to thaw almost any frozen cake with few exceptions, but with care even these may be successfully accomplished. One of the exceptions is where a cake has been filled or decorated with fresh cream, or butter cream, in which case it is likely that the cream will thaw more rapidly than the cake itself. Therefore, it is wiser not to thaw in the oven.

To thaw a 20 cm (8 inch) cake it is only necessary to subject it to about 3 minutes of microwave energy and then leave it to stand for 5 minutes before serving. If it is not quite thawed, pop it back in the oven for a minute or two.

Small fairy-type cakes only take about 30 seconds and then should be left to stand for 2 minutes. If a number of small cakes are in the oven being thawed the time is increased, but as soon as any one small cake feels warm to the touch, it should be removed immediately.

## Eggs and Cheese

Both eggs and cheese require special care when cooked in a microwave oven as these foods cook in such a very short time that seconds can make all the difference to the end result. If they are overcooked they will become tough and rubbery.

When cooking eggs and egg dishes, it is better to err on the side of undercooking and allow the heat within the food gently to finish the process. In general, it is better to use eggs at room temperature rather than from the refrigerator. If the egg is to be 'fried' or 'poached', the egg yolk should be pricked with a cocktail stick to prevent it losing its domed shape.

Scrambled eggs are a delight to cook as the texture can be varied to suit every taste, ranging from a wet creamy mixture to a solid mass. To achieve this, it is simply a question of removing the mixture from the dish at the desired time.

To scramble two eggs: the eggs, melted butter, seasoning and milk are lightly beaten together and put in an uncovered, non-metallic container, such as a soup dish. They are cooked for about 1 minute, the mixture is then stirred, and returned to the oven for a minute or so. If more eggs are to be scrambled and a deeper container used, then the times should be increased accordingly.

Dishes made with cheese are always very tasty and popular and the microwave oven manufacturer's recipe books do include a range that will appeal to most people. However, if a golden finish is required, it will be necessary to put the made dish under a hot preheated grill. Fondue is easily made in the oven.

## Fish

To cook fish from the raw state is both fast and simple. If, for example, a 500 g (1 lb) quantity is to be cooked, just brush the fish with melted unsalted butter, sprinkle with pepper to taste, place it in a shallow, non-metallic container and cover or wrap in cling film. Cook for approximately 6 minutes. A thick slice should be turned over half way during the cooking period.

Thawing frozen fish presents no difficulties and fillets can be thawed in seconds. As fish thaws so quickly, it is usually better partially to thaw it and to give short bursts of micro-wave energy and short rest periods. As this type of operation is so quick, it is advisable to cook the fish immediately it has been thawed.

## Fruit

Both fresh and frozen fruit can be thawed, heated and cooked without losing their original shape and colour, and in many instances the addition of water is not necessary. This is especially so when frozen fruits are being thawed as there will be sufficient moisture from the melted ice. Whether thawing, heating, or cooking it is better to undercook and allow the fruit to finish off cooking by using its own heat.

When thawing frozen fruit it is wise to check its condition fairly frequently and, to aid the thawing process, the fruit can be gently separated with a fork during the operation. The thawing time is very fast, taking only something like 2–3 minutes to thaw a 250 g (8 oz) quantity. A better method is to partially thaw the fruit and then allow it to stand for a few minutes before serving.

Prepare fresh fruit for cooking by the usual methods – wash, peel, core and stone, if necessary, and slice or chop. Sugar or any flavouring can be sprinkled over the fruit. The fruit should be stirred once during the operation. Cooking time for hard fruits will be about 8–10 minutes, and for softer fruits 3–5 minutes. Whole fruit cannot be stirred so turn the container during cooking to ensure that the fruit is evenly cooked.

Fruit, such as baked apples, which may be cooked in their skins, should be pricked, cut or pierced. This helps to prevent the fruit bursting during the cooking process.


## Meat and Poultry

On the whole both fresh meat and poultry should always be thawed before cooking to ensure the best result. However, if the quantity is very small the thawing and cooking may be carried out almost simultaneously. The cooking time given in this book must only be taken as approximate and the microwave oven manufacturer's recipe book should always be referred to.

Avoid seasoning meat and poultry with salt, as this absorbs the moisture and can toughen the outer surface of the food. Add any seasoning after cooking has finished.

The exterior appearance of meat and poultry cooked in a microwave oven can be deceptive as it may look cooked when in fact the interior is undercooked. It is, therefore, important to follow the manufacturer's instructions on cooking times, and it is better to undercook meat and poultry rather than overcook, to avoid the food drying out.

Meat and poultry can be roasted in a non-metallic dish with a covering to avoid undue splashing of the fats and juices, but the use of a roasting bag would be preferable. To protect the thin end of a joint, or wings of poultry from becoming overcooked, wrap in foil then place the food in a bag, securing the end with a piece of string. Make a small slit in the bag to allow the steam to escape, and place in a dish to cook for the appropriate cooking time.

Halfway through the cooking time drain off the juices and turn the joint or poultry over. When you take the meat or poultry out of the oven remove the roasting bag and wrap the meat in foil with shiny side inside and leave to stand for about

15–20 minutes. This allows the heat within the joint or poultry to be conducted right through to the very centre, so that when it is carved it will be succulent and hot to eat.

A basic microwave oven is not able to produce a crisp brown appearance on smaller cuts of meat or poultry. If this is required, the food may be either quickly browned under a preheated grill, lightly fried in a pan before or after cooking, or a microwave oven browning plate can be used. (See pages 16 and 32.)

The easiest joint to roast is one which has been boned and rolled, as this gives an even thickness of solid meat. But meat or poultry on the bone can also be cooked most successfully.

The method of cooking meat and poultry is slightly different to conventional cooking. The cooking time per pound is also very much shorter, as can be seen in the following table:

Table 3. Meat chart: times are given per 500 grammes (1 lb)

| Meat | Rare Minutes | Medium Minutes | Well done Minutes |
|---|---|---|---|
| Beef boned | 6–7 | 7–8½ | 8½–10 |
| With bone | 5½–6½ | 6½–7½ | 7½–9 |
| Lamb (leg or shoulder) | | 7 | 8–8½ |
| Pork (shoulder) | | | 10–13 |
| Veal (rolled) | | | 10–11½ |
| Poultry | | | 6–8 |

Thawing meat takes about 2 minutes per 500 g (1 lb) and poultry 2–3 minutes for 500 g (1 lb). Both meat and poultry should be turned over halfway through the operation. Then remove from the microwave oven and allow it to stand for about 15–20 minutes before cooking.

Most microwave oven manufacturers will advise the user to carry out the operation in stages by subjecting the meat to bursts of microwave energy, e.g. two minutes on and two minutes off. So far as smaller cuts of meat are concerned, such as a piece of steak, the thawing time may be shortened as the need to use any spread of heat (see page 31) is reduced due to the thickness of the meat being less. To retain the thawed meat juices, the joint can be placed on an upturned saucer which will collect any juices from the meat.


## Pastry

Cooking raw pastry in a microwave oven is not always successful and it may be better to cook it by conventional methods. But short crust pastry, strudel pastry and suet pastry are relatively successful cooked as open flan cases or as a strudel dish.

Fruit pies, which use a double crust, are not successful because the filling tends to cook and bubble over before the pastry has cooked.

It is possible to cook small pieces of puff pastry and the like by turning them over during the cooking period, when a light and flaky pastry will result.

It is worth carrying out some experiments to establish whether or not the end result is acceptable and to be aware that pastry cooked in a microwave oven will not be browned.

A shortcrust 150 mm (6 inch) pastry flan will take about 4 minutes to cook. The method of preparing the container is a matter of choice. An uncovered non-metallic plate pie dish may be lined with the pastry which needs to be well pricked to avoid bubbling. However, a better result may be achieved by lining the container with the pastry, placing a piece of absorbent paper over it, and putting a slightly smaller plate or pie dish on top of the pastry. After about 2½ minutes cooking, remove both the retaining dish and paper and return the flan in its original container to the oven to cook for a further minute or two. Any flan case can be used to accommodate fillings and the microwave oven may be used to cook them most successfully.

Biscuit crust flans are very satisfactory and simple to make in the microwave oven. Melt the butter in the oven. Remove and add the crushed biscuits and press them into shape in the flan dish. In the space of a minute or two it will be cooked.

Home-made tarts can be cooked and frozen in advance, then quickly thawed. Simply place the tart on absorbent paper, and use short bursts of microwave energy.

### Pasta, Rice, Cereals

*Pasta*. Pasta may be cooked in the microwave oven but the time taken is almost the same as for conventional methods. However, the microwave oven is a quick and easy way to reheat spaghetti, macaroni or noodles.

To cook pasta a broad rule of thumb is to every two cups of pasta use six cups of water, adding a pinch of salt and a dash of cooking oil.

The non-metallic container used should be large enough to hold the contents without 'boiling over' occurring. Whether or not the container is covered depends on individual oven manufacturers' recommendations. If a cover is used, it should fit loosely to allow steam to escape.

After cooking the container should be removed from the oven and left to stand covered for at least ten minutes.

To reheat pasta, whether it has been refrigerated or not, simply place it in a lightly covered container and heat it until it is steaming. During the reheating period it is advisable to stir the pasta at least once.

*Rice*. Rice, like pasta, may be cooked by either the conventional cooking method or in the microwave oven but again the microwave oven is particularly useful for reheating purposes.

It is advisable to refer to the manufacturer's recipe book for cooking instructions. A quick guide would be about one cup of rice to two cups of water.

The non-metallic container should be large enough to hold the rice and water with ease. It should be lightly covered during the cooking process to allow the steam to escape.

In general, quick cooking rice is put into boiling water, whereas the conventional rice is put into cold water. Whichever type of rice is being cooked, it must always be removed from the oven and left to stand in the covered container after cooking for at least eight minutes. After the standing period, the rice should be fluffed up with a fork before serving and, if necessary, reheated.

The method of reheating rice is exactly the same as for pasta.

Frozen rice dishes may be thawed in a covered container. The container is placed in the oven for about 5 minutes for a 300 g (10 oz) quantity, at which point remove the container from the oven and break up the rice with a fork. Return it to the oven for a further two minutes, remove and stir again, and allow to stand covered for approximately two minutes before serving.

*Cereals.* Place the cereal into an appropriate dish and stir in the liquid. Cook for a minute or two, remove from the oven and stir. It should then be ready to eat. If larger quantities are required, a large non-metallic uncovered container should be used and the cereal stirred once or twice during cooking.


**Puddings and Desserts**

The range of puddings and desserts which may be cooked in a microwave oven is almost endless. Most microwave oven manufacturers' recipe books give a large variety and include dishes such as upside-down cakes, bread puddings, fruit crumbles, dumplings, cheese cakes, suet puddings, crème caramels and mousses. Therefore, it is difficult to give general guidelines as to the shape, size and covering requirements of the container. However, if the moisture in the food is to be retained, the container should be covered. Remember, it is also possible to use the same dish for cooking and serving the food.

The principle of thawing frozen desserts and puddings is simple. Give the food short bursts of microwave energy followed by a standing period to allow the heat within the food to continue the thawing process while resting.

A pudding or dessert is often made one day and eaten the next, but the beauty of a microwave oven is its ability to allow the housewife to reheat the whole dish or to serve either hot

4

or cold individual portions depending upon the family's preference.


## Soups

Soups, using fresh ingredients, can be made in the microwave oven, tinned soups can be reheated, dehydrated soups can be reconstituted and reheated; and frozen soups may be thawed and reheated.

The uncovered non-metallic container should be large enough to contain the liquid and to prevent boiling over. The soup should be stirred once or twice during the heating period.

It is often quicker to heat the soup in the serving dishes or mugs and take them straight to the table. The soup can also be heated in a non-metallic tureen and served from this.

The heating time, which is only a few minutes, will depend on the initial temperature of the soup and the size of the container.

After heating, dehydrated soups should be left to stand for about 5 minutes before serving, but as there are numerous types on the market this time may need adjustment. It is, however, likely that with these soups the conventional method of heating would be preferred.

To thaw frozen soups use an uncovered non-metallic container. During thawing and heating the soup should be broken up with a fork and stirred occasionally. The time taken will depend on the type and quantity of the soup but it will only be a few minutes.


## Sauces

Sauces are simple and quick to make in the microwave oven and there is little chance of burning or scorching them. Sauces which have been cooked the day before and refrigerated may be quickly reheated for serving or frozen sauces can be thawed and reheated in a matter of minutes.

The container in which the sauce is made should be large enough to contain the liquid without boiling over. Cooking is carried out in an uncovered container. The following examples give an idea of how easy it is to make a sauce in a microwave oven:

*Chocolate sauce.* Melted chocolate, water, syrup and evaporated milk are combined together before placing in the oven.

*Jam sauce.* Jam and a little water are heated together.

*Quick caramel sauce.* Melt some caramel sweets in the oven.

*Basic white sauce.* Melt the butter in a container in the microwave oven, remove and blend in the flour and milk. Return to the oven and cook for about 3 minutes, giving the mixture a stir about every minute for a 250 ml ($\frac{1}{2}$ pint approximately) quantity.

To thaw frozen sauces use a covered non-metallic container and follow the same method as for soups.


### Vegetables

Most vegetables, whether tinned, frozen or fresh, can be thawed, reheated or cooked quickly in a microwave oven. The speed of the operation helps to retain the colour and nutrients. As little, if any, water is used the vegetables remain crisp. Frozen vegetables are unlikely to need any extra liquid as there will be sufficient for cooking purposes as the ice melts.

When heating tinned vegetables pour off the liquid.

An indication of the quantities of liquid required for fresh vegetables is given in Table 4. It is only intended as a guide and the individual manufacturer's recipe book should be referred to.

Fresh, frozen or tinned vegetables will cook, or heat up more evenly if covered. So always cover the non-metallic container but not too tightly as the steam needs to escape. The contents should be stirred at least once during the

# Table 4. Water requirements for fresh vegetables

| Vegetable | Quantity | Water |
|---|---|---|
| Artichokes | 4 medium | 375 ml (12 fl.oz approx.) |
| Asparagus | 12 stalks | 75 ml (3 fl.oz approx.) |
| Runner beans | 500 grams (1 lb approx.) | 75 ml (3 fl.oz approx.) |
| Beetroots | 4 medium | Cover with water |
| Broccoli | 500 grams (1 lb approx.) | 75 ml (3 fl.oz approx.) |
| Brussels sprouts | 500 grams (1 lb approx.) | 40 ml (1½ fl.oz approx.) |
| Cabbage | 1 medium | 75 ml (3 fl.oz approx.) |
| Carrots | 6 medium | 75 ml (3 fl.oz approx.) |
| Cauliflower | 1 medium | 40 ml (1½ fl.oz approx.) |
| Aubergine | 500 grams (1 lb approx.) | 75 ml (3 fl.oz approx.) |
| Mushrooms | 500 grams (1 lb approx.) | 40 ml (1½ fl.oz approx.) |
| Small onions | 500 grams (1 lb approx.) | None |
| Parsnips | 4 medium | 75 ml (3 fl.oz approx.) |
| Peas | 1 kg (2 lb approx.) | 40 ml (1½ fl.oz approx.) |
| Potatoes (boiled) | Any quantity | Cover with water |
| Spinach | 500 grams (1 lb approx.) | With water that clings to the leaves |

operation. It is important not to overcook as vegetables quickly dehydrate and become tough as a result. This is particularly the case with vegetables which have a high starch content, such as potatoes.

Any salt or seasoning should be put in the bottom of the container rather than sprinkled over the vegetables themselves as this tends to dehydrate them. The salt will season all the vegetables as they are stirred during the cooking operation.

Frozen vegetables may be defrosted and cooked in one operation. Tinned vegetables simply need reheating. It is difficult to give specific cooking times as the age, freshness and quality can have a bearing on the cooking time. Nevertheless, the following Tables 5 and 6 are a guide to the sort of times which could be expected.

When cooking vegetables in their skins, gently prick or pierce the skin to prevent the vegetable bursting during cooking.

Jacket potatoes can be cooked in minutes. Scrub and prick them, arrange them on absorbent paper, allowing a space between each and place in the oven. Turn them round half way during the cooking period.

# Table 5. Cooking and heating guide

| Product | Quantity | Application | Preparation | Water added | Stir/ shake | Time |
|---------|----------|-------------|-------------|-------------|-------------|------|
| Apple sauce | 6 | Cooking | Peel, core and cut | Yes | Yes | 8 min |
| Beans (green) | 10 oz (300 g) | Cooking | Cut in small pieces—cook | Yes | Yes | 10 min |
| Beans (green) | 14 oz (450 g) | Heating | Open can | Yes | Yes | 4 min |
| Broccoli | 8 oz (250 g) | Heating | Heat—covered | No | Yes | 2¼ min |
| Broccoli | 8 oz (250 g) | Cooking | Cook—wrapped in cellophane | No | Yes | 9 min |
| Brussels sprouts | 16 oz (500 g) | Cooking | Clean, cook—covered | Yes | Yes | 12 min |
| Brussels sprouts | 7 oz (200 g) | Heating | Heat—covered | No | Yes | 5 min |
| Cabbage (white) | 16 oz (500 g) | Cooking | Cut and cook—covered | Yes | Yes | 12 min |
| Cabbage (white) | 16 oz (500 g) | Heating | Heat—covered | No | Yes | 6 min |
| Carrots | 14 oz (450 g) | Cooking | Cut in slices, cook—covered | Yes | Yes | 14 min |
| Carrots | 14 oz (450 g) | Heating | Heat—covered | No | Yes | 4 min |
| Cauliflower | 14 oz (450 g) | Cooking | Make roses, cook—covered | Yes | Yes | 15 min |
| Cauliflower | 14 oz (450 g) | Heating | Heat—covered | No | Yes | 3 min |
| Celery | 10 oz (300 g) | Heating | Heat—covered | No | Yes | 4 min |
| Chicory | 10 oz (300 g) | Cooking | Cook—covered | Yes | Yes | 11 min |
| Chicory | 10 oz (300 g) | Heating | Heat—covered | No | Yes | 4 min |
| Corn-on-the-cob | 1 | Cooking | Cook wrapped in cellophane | Yes | No | 7 min |
| Corn (cut) | 12 oz (350 g) | Heating | Heat—covered | No | Yes | 3 min |
| Cucumber | 10 oz (300 g) | Cooking | Peel, cut in pieces, cook—covered | Yes | Yes | 5 min |
| Leeks | 16 oz (500 g) | Cooking | Cut thinly, cook—covered | Yes | Yes | 15 min |
| Peas | 14 oz (450 g) | Heating | Heat—covered | Yes | Yes | 3¼ min |
| Potatoes | 16 oz (500 g) | Cooking | Peel, cut, cook—covered | Yes | Yes | 15 min |
| Spinach | 16 oz (500 g) | Cooking | Cook—covered with water that clings to the leaves | No | Yes | 7 min |
| Sweet pepper | 2 halves | Cooking | Cook—covered | Yes | Yes | 5 min |
| *Miscellaneous* | | | | | | |
| 3 component meal | 16 oz (500g) | Heating | Heat—covered | No | Yes | 4¼ min |
| Soup | 1 cup | Heating | Heat—uncovered | No | Yes | 90 sec |
| Milk | 1 glass | Heating | Heat—uncovered | No | Yes | 30/40sec |
| Chocolate | 1 glass | Heating | Mix ingredients, heat uncovered | No | Yes | 90 sec |
| Coffee/tea | 1 cup | Heating | Boil water add coffee or tea | No | Yes | 1½ min |
| Ragoûts/stews | 8 oz (250 g) | Heating | Heat—covered | No | Yes | 3 min |
| Rice | 16 oz (500 g) | Heating | Heat—covered | No | Yes | 4 min |
| Mashed potatoes | 14 oz (450 g) | Heating | Heat—covered | No | Yes | 5 min |

# Table 6. Frozen food cooking guide

| Food | Quantity | Application | Preparation | Water added | Stir/ shake/ turn | Time |
|------|----------|-------------|-------------|-------------|-------------------|------|
| Apple sauce | 14 oz (450 g) | Defrosting | Heat—uncovered | No | Yes | 10 min |
| Beans (green) | 10 oz (300g) | Defrosting + cooking | Small pieces wrapped in cellophane, cook—covered | Yes | Yes | 12 min |
| Broccoli | 10 oz (300 g) | Defrosting + cooking | Wrap in cellophane cook—covered | Yes | Yes | 12 min |
| Brussels sprouts | 7 oz (175 g) | Defrosting + cooking | Cook—covered | Yes | Yes | 9 min |
| Cabbage | 14 oz (450 g) | Defrosting + cooking | Cook—covered | No | Yes | 12 min |
| Carrots | 10 oz (300 g) | Defrosting + cooking | Cook—covered | Yes | Yes | 14 min |
| Cauliflower | 14 oz (450 g) | Defrosting + cooking | Cook—covered | Yes | Yes | 12 min |
| Corn | 13 oz (425 g) | Defrosting + cooking | Cook—covered | Yes | Yes | 11 min |
| Mixed vegetables | 8 oz (250 g) | Defrosting + cooking | Cook—covered | Yes | Yes | 9 min |
| Peas | 8 oz (250 g) | Defrosting + cooking | Cook—covered | Yes | Yes | 9 min |
| Peas and carrots | 8 oz (250 g) | Defrosting + cooking | Cook—covered | Yes | Yes | 9 min |
| Spinach | 13 oz (425 g) | Defrosting + cooking | Cook—covered | Yes | Yes | 8 min |
| *Miscellaneous* | | | | | | |
| Bread, slice | | Defrosting | Uncovered | No | No | 30 sec |
| Bread, loaf | | Defrosting with intervals | Uncovered | No | Yes | 3 min |
| Cake, slice | | Defrosting | Uncovered | No | No | 40 sec |
| Fruits | 14 oz (450 g) | Defrosting with intervals | Uncovered | No | Yes | 8 min |
| Mashed potatoes | 16 oz (500 g) | Defrosting + heating | Covered | No | Yes | 9 min |
| Chicken ragoût | 15 oz (475 g) | Defrosting | Covered | No | Yes | 10 min |
| Complete meals | 16 oz (500 g) | Defrosting + heating | Covered | No | Yes | 7–10 min |
| Rice | 16 oz (500 g) | Defrosting + heating | Covered | No | Yes | 10 min |

# Chapter 7

# Using the Recipe Section

### Important

All the recipe instructions given in this section are designed for microwave cookery. However, it is important to check that the instructions given in your microwave oven instruction manual are similar.

The recipes in this book have been tested but the times given will be influenced by:

1) the condition, temperature and structure of the food;
2) the container being used;
3) the output of the oven in use.

To help you to use your recipes with ease a space has been included for you to enter the cooking times which you find to be right for your own oven.

Each recipe also indicates the course it is most suitable for, how long the oven is in use, serving suggestions, and whether the dish can be prepared in advance.

The recipes have been designed to take into account the convenience of today's food and the convenience of the microwave oven. It is hoped that by combining the two the cook may become even more creative without having to surrender too much of her time.

### Note:

★ The recipes are for four servings.

★ The oven used to test the recipes had an output of 700 watts.

## The Quantities

Two types of measurements have been given, the imperial in pounds, and ounces, and pints, and the metric in grammes, kilogrammes, millilitres and centimetres. It is important that you follow only one type of measurement and do not work in the two systems. In case you are using cookbooks giving American cup measurements, some of these are also given.

## Conversion Tables

### Table 7.

| Weight Imperial | Exact conversions | Metric equivalent used |
|---|---|---|
| 1 oz | 28.35 g | 25 g |
| 8 oz | 226.8 g | 250 g |
| 1 lb | 453.6 g | 500 g |
| 2 lb | 907.2 g | 1 kg |
| *Liquid* (One teaspoon = 1 x 5 ml spoon) (One table spoon = 1 x 15 ml spoon) | | |
| 1 fl oz | 28.35 ml | 25 ml |
| 5 fl oz | 141.75 ml | 125 ml |
| 10 fl oz (½ pint) | 283.50 ml | 250 ml |
| 1 pint | 567 ml | 500 ml or ½ litre |
| 1¾ pints | 992.25 ml | 1 litre |
| *Length* | | |
| 1 in | 2.54 cm | 2.5 cm (250 mm) |
| 2 in | 5.08 cm | 5.0 cm (500 mm) |
| 3 in | 7.62 cm | 7.5 cm (750 mm) |
| 4 in | 10.16 cm | 10.0 cm (1000 mm) |
| 5 in | 12.70 cm | 12.5 cm (1125 mm) |
| 6 in | 15.20 cm | 15.0 cm (1150 mm) |

### Table 8.

| Food | American Cup | British Cup |
|---|---|---|
| Dried fruit, raisins | 5 oz (125 g) | 6 oz (150 g) |
| Flour | 4 oz (100 g) | 5 oz (125 g) |
| Syrup | 12 oz (300 g) | 14 oz (450 g) |
| Icing sugar | 4½ oz (112 g) | 5 oz (125 g) |
| Fats e.g. butter | 8 oz (250 g) | 8 oz (250 g) |

*Note:* 1 American pint = 16 fl oz
1 British pint = 20 fl oz (500 ml or ½ litre)

# Recipes

## POTATO AND ONION SOUP

**INGREDIENTS**

4 oz (100 g) butter
3 medium size onions
2 tablespoons (30ml) instant potato
2 beef stock cubes
1½ pints (750 ml) boiling water
Pepper to taste
Garnish: chopped chives

*Microwave oven in use
for 9 minutes*

**METHOD**

| | Approximate cooking time | Your cooking time |
|---|---|---|
| 1) Cube the butter and place into a large bowl. Melt butter for ... | 1 minute | |
| 2) Peel and slice the onions. Stir into the butter the peeled and sliced onions and cover the bowl. Return to the oven to cook for ... After 2 and 4 minutes stir the onions. | 5 minutes | |
| 3) Remove the bowl from the oven and stir in the potato, stock cubes and the boiling water. | | |
| 4) Cover the bowl, return to the oven and cook for ... ... ... | 3 minutes | |
| 5) Adjust the seasoning if necessary and pour into the serving bowls. | | |

*Serving Suggestions.* Garnish with chopped chives. Serve hot with french bread.

*Can be Made in Advance.* Suitable to refrigerate overnight or for freezing.

# SPINACH SOUP

### INGREDIENTS

1 oz (25 g) flour
10 oz (300 g) drained tinned spinach
¾ pint (375 ml) chicken stock
½ pint (250 ml) milk
Pepper to taste
Garnish: chopped parsley

> Microwave oven in use
> for 9 minutes

### METHOD

1) In a large bowl stir the flour into the spinach and then add the remaining ingredients. Cover bowl. Cook for ... ... ... Stir after 5 minutes.

2) Allow soup to stand for 1 minute before blending in a blender or passing through a sieve.

3) Pour into 4 serving bowls.

| Approximate cooking time | Your cooking time |
|---|---|
| 9 minutes | |

*Serving Suggestions.* Garnish with chopped parsley. Serve hot with french bread.

*Can be Made in Advance.* Suitable to refrigerate overnight or for freezing.

## MUSHROOM SOUP

INGREDIENTS
8 oz (250 g) mushrooms
2 oz (50 g) butter
2 oz (50 g) flour
½ pint (250 ml) chicken stock
½ pint (250 ml) milk
Salt and pepper to taste
Garnish: thin slices of mushrooms

> Microwave oven in use
> for 10 minutes

METHOD

| | Approximate cooking time | Your cooking time |
|---|---|---|
| 1) Peel and chop the mushrooms. Cut the butter into four and place, with the mushrooms, into a large bowl. Cover. Cook for ...  ... | 3 minutes | |
| 2) Stir in flour and gradually add the stock and milk. Return to the oven uncovered to cook for ... Stir after approximately every 2 minutes. | 7 minutes | |
| 3) Stir, season to taste. Pour into soup bowls. | | |

*Serving Suggestions.* Garnish with thin slices of mushroom. Serve hot with french bread.

*Can be Made in Advance.* Suitable to refrigerate overnight or for freezing.

# LETTUCE SOUP

INGREDIENTS
6 oz (150 g) lettuce leaves
1 medium size onion
2 oz (50 g) butter
¾ pint (375 ml) hot water
1 chicken stock cube
½ pint (250 ml) cold milk
A good pinch marjoram
Salt and pepper to taste
1 oz (25 g) instant potato
1 egg yolk
Garnish: fried *croûtons*

> Microwave oven in use
> for 12½ minutes

METHOD

1) Wash, drain and chop the lettuce. Peel and finely dice the onion.

| Method step | Approximate cooking time | Your cooking time |
|---|---|---|
| 2) Cut the butter into knobs and place into a large bowl. Melt the butter for ... ... ... ... | 1½ minutes | |
| 3) Add the onion. Cover the bowl and cook for ... ... ... | 3 minutes | |
| 4) Stir in the lettuce, hot water, stock cube, milk, marjoram and salt and pepper. Return to the oven. Cook for ... ... ... ... Stir after 3 and 6 minutes. | 8 minutes | |

5) Remove the soup, stir in the instant potato and pour into a blender.

6) Add the egg yolk and blend the ingredients together, until the lettuce is finely chopped. Adjust the seasoning.

*Serving Suggestions.* Serve with *croûtons*.

*Can be Made in Advance.* Suitable to refrigerate overnight or for freezing.

# CHILLED COURGETTE SOUP Starter

INGREDIENTS

1 lb (500 g) courgettes
1 medium size onion
1 chicken stock cube
A good pinch dried mint
Salt and pepper to taste
¾ pint (375 ml) boiling water
1 oz (25 g) cornflour
½ pint (250 ml) milk
¼ pint (125 ml) cream
Garnish: a few very finely sliced
pieces of courgette. Mint.

| | Microwave oven in use for 12 minutes |

METHOD

1) Wash, trim off the ends and very finely slice the courgettes. Peel and finely dice the onion.

2) Place the vegetables in a large bowl with the stock cube, mint, salt, pepper and boiling water. Cook for ...   ...   ...   ...   ... Stir occasionally.

3) Remove from the oven and leave to stand.

4) Blend the cornflour with the milk in a jug. Cook for...   ...   ... Stir after 1 minute.

5) Mix the cornflour liquid with the courgettes. Leave to cool.

6) Blend in a blender.

| Approximate cooking time | Your cooking time |
|---|---|
| 10 minutes | |
| 2 minutes | |

*Serving Suggestions.* When cold stir in the cream and refrigerate until ready to serve. Serve garnished with one or two very fine slices of courgette and mint.

*Can be Made in Advance.* Suitable for freezing or to refrigerate overnight but in both cases add the cream before serving. Should a thinner soup be required, add more cream.

# ANCHOVY SCRAMBLED EGGS

### INGREDIENTS
4 slices bread
4 oz (100 g) butter
4 large eggs
4 tablespoons (60 ml) milk
Salt and pepper
Garnish: 1 tin anchovies and sprigs
of parsley

> *Microwave oven in use for 4½ minutes*

### METHOD

|  | Approximate cooking time | Your cooking time |
|---|---|---|
| 1) Cut bread into large rounds and fry or toast. Keep warm. | | |
| 2) Cut butter into 4 and place into a large jug or mixing bowl. Melt for ... ... ... ... ... | 1 minute | |
| 3) Beat into butter the eggs, milk and seasoning and cover the container. Return to oven to cook for ... Stir mixture after 2 minutes. | 3 minutes | |
| 4) Return to the oven for ... ... Stir after a further 1 minute of cooking. If necessary return to the oven for a further 30 seconds. | 30 seconds | |
| 5) Divide the mixture over the four slices of fried bread. | | |

*Serving Suggestions.* Drain the anchovies and arrange these over the scrambled eggs. Garnish with sprigs of parsley.

*Can be Made in Advance.* Not advisable.

## HOT CRAB IN CASES Starter

INGREDIENTS

1 oz (25 g) butter
4 or 8 ready-made *vol-au-vent* cases
½ pt (250 ml) milk
1 oz (25 g) flour
1 egg, beaten
Salt and pepper
1 tin crab meat
Garnish: parsley and lemon

| Microwave oven in use for 5¼ minutes |
| --- |

METHOD

| | Approximate cooking time | Your cooking time |
| --- | --- | --- |
| 1) Put the butter in a jug and place in oven to melt for ... ... ... | 30 seconds | |
| 2) Remove butter and stir in the flour and milk. Cook for ... ... | 3 minutes | |
| 3) Stir every minute. | | |
| 4) Beat in egg, season to taste, stir in drained crab meat. Heat for ... | 1 minute | |
| 5) Heat *vol-au-vent* cases if desired in oven for... ... ... ... | 1 minute | |
| 6) Pile crab mixture into cases. | | |

*Serving Suggestions.* Serve on a bed of lettuce. Garnish with parsley and lemon.

*Can be Made in Advance.* Cases may be cooked and frozen. Sauce may be made earlier, refrigerated and reheated when required.

# POTTED SHRIMPS

INGREDIENTS

6 oz (150 g) butter
12 oz (300 g) peeled shrimps
A pinch cayenne
Salt and pepper to taste
Garnish: lettuce and lemon wedges

METHOD

1) Cut butter into 4 and place in a
   bowl. Melt for   ...   ...   ...
   Check at 1¼ minutes.

2) Mix the shrimps into the melted
   butter and season to taste.

3) Pour the mixture into 4 small
   dishes and leave to set.

4) Turn out before serving.

| Microwave oven in use for 2½ minutes | |
|---|---|
| Approximate cooking time | Your cooking time |
| 2½ minutes | |

*Serving Suggestions.* Serve on a bed of lettuce with lemon wedges.
Hand hot toast separately.

*Can be Made in Advance.* Suitable to refrigerate overnight or for
freezing.

5

## TROUT

INGREDIENTS
4 trout
Melted unsalted butter
Garnish: parsley and lemon wedges

METHOD

| | Microwave oven in use for 10 minutes | |
|---|---|---|
| | *Approximate cooking time* | *Your cooking time* |

1) Wash and clean trout. Brush each with melted butter.

2) Arrange on dish and cover. Cook for ...    ...    ...    ...    ...    **5 minutes**

3) Turn dish and cook for a further... **5 minutes**

4) Remove trout from oven and allow to stand 2 minutes before serving.

*Serving Suggestions.* Serve with toast. Garnish with lemon wedges and parsley.

*Can be Made in Advance.* Not advised.

# HOT SARDINES WITH LEMON

INGREDIENTS
8 large tinned sardines
Juice and grated rind of 1 lemon
Pepper to taste
Garnish: lemon and parsley

| Microwave oven in use for 2 minutes | |
|---|---|
| Approximate cooking time | Your cooking time |

METHOD

1) Drain and mash the sardines. Season with pepper, grated rind and juice of lemon, and arrange on flat dish.

2) Cover. Heat for ...    ...    ...

3) Remove from oven and stand 1–2 minutes before serving.

2 minutes

*Serving Suggestions.* Spread on to rounds of hot buttered toast. Garnish with lemon and parsley.

*Can be Made in Advance.* Not advised.

INGREDIENTS

8 oz (250 g) cooked chicken
1 envelope gelatine
¾ pint (375 ml) water
1 teaspoon (5 ml) meat extract
Salt and pepper to taste
Garnish: lettuce

| | |
|---|---|
| *Microwave oven in use for 2½ minutes* | |

METHOD

| Approximate cooking time | Your cooking time |
|---|---|

1) Dice or chop chicken and arrange in the base of a mould.

2) Put the gelatine in a jug and stir in half of the water. Dissolve the gelatine for...  ...  ...  ... **2½ minutes**
Stir thoroughly after 1 and 2 minutes.

3) Remove the jelly and stir in the meat extract, and the remainder of the cold water.

4) Season to taste if desired with salt and pepper.

5) Leave to cool and then pour over the chicken.

6) Allow the jelly to set in a refrigerator if possible.

*Serving Suggestions.* Serve with toast. Turn out and garnish with lettuce.

*Can be Made in Advance.* Suitable to refrigerate.

# SMOOTH PÂTÉ

INGREDIENTS

1 medium size onion
¾ lb (375 g) chicken livers
3 oz (75 g) butter
1 teaspoon (5 ml) mixed herbs
Garlic salt and pepper
2 tablespoons (30 ml) brandy (optional)
A pinch mustard
Garnish: lettuce and tomatoes

| | Microwave oven in use for 9 minutes |

METHOD

| | Approximate cooking time | Your cooking time |
|---|---|---|
| 1) Peel and finely chop the onions. Chop the livers. | | |
| 2) Cut butter into knobs and place in a bowl. Melt butter for ... ... | 1 minute | |
| 3) Add onions and cover bowl. Cook for ... ... ... ... ... | 3 minutes | |
| 4) Add livers, herbs, seasonings and brandy. Cover bowl and cook for ... ... ... ... ... | 5 minutes | |
| 5) Pour mixture into blender. Blend until smooth. | | |
| 6) Pour pâté into 4 individual dishes or large dish. | | |

*Serving Suggestions.* Serve with hot toast. Garnish with lettuce and tomatoes.

*Can be Made in Advance.* Suitable to refrigerate overnight or for freezing.

INGREDIENTS
4 small frankfurters
1 large tin potato salad
Garnish: sliced or quartered tomatoes

METHOD

1) Place the frankfurters on a piece
   of absorbent paper in a flat dish.
   Heat for ... ... ... ...

2) Check if ready at 1 minute. If not
   continue heating for ... ...

| Microwave oven in use for 1½ minutes | |
| --- | --- |
| Approximate cooking time | Your cooking time |
| 1½ minutes | |
| 30 seconds | |

*Serving Suggestions.* Arrange on a bed of potato salad. Garnish with sliced or quartered tomatoes.

*Can be Made in Advance.* Not advisable.

INGREDIENTS

2 grapefruit
4 teaspoons (20 ml) sherry (optional)
4 teaspoons (20 ml) demerara sugar
¼ teaspoon (1 ml) cinnamon
4 teaspoons (20 ml) castor sugar (if desired)
4 small knobs unsalted butter
Decoration: 4 Maraschino cherries

Microwave oven in use for 5 minutes

METHOD

1) Cut the grapefruit in half, segment by removing the core, skin and pips. Place grapefruits into serving dishes.

2) Mix together the sherry, demerara sugar and cinnamon.

3) Pour the sugar mixture over each half and place a knob of butter on each. Heat uncovered for...   ...

4) Sprinkle with castor sugar if desired.

| Approximate cooking time | Your cooking time |
|---|---|
| 5 minutes | |

*Serving Suggestions.* Serve hot decorated with a cherry.

*Can be Made in Advance.* Not advisable.

INGREDIENTS
4 medium size potatoes
3 oz (75 g) corned beef (cubed)
1 tablespoon (15 ml) tomato sauce
Salt and pepper to taste
1 tablespoon (15 ml) milk or cream
Garnish: sprigs of parsley

> *Microwave oven in use for 12 minutes*

METHOD

| | Approximate cooking time | Your cooking time |
|---|---|---|
| 1) Wash and dry potatoes, prick each with fork. Place potatoes on to absorbent paper in the oven. Cook for ... ... ... ... | 6 minutes | |
| 2) Turn each potato over and cook for a further ... ... ... | 6 minutes | |
| 3) Remove potatoes from oven and wrap in foil. Leave to stand for 5 minutes. | | |
| 4) Slit the top of each potato, remove contents and mash with the remaining ingredients. | | |
| 5) Pile potato/corned beef mixture into the potato skins. If necessary return to the oven to reheat for... | 2-3 minutes | |

*Serving Suggestions*. Garnish with sprigs of parsley.

*Can be Made in Advance*. Not advisable.

## BUTTERED CORN

INGREDIENTS
4 frozen corn on the cob
Melted unsalted butter
Garnish: sprigs of parsley

METHOD

1) Brush corn with melted butter.

2) Wrap in greaseproof paper and arrange in dish.

3) Cook the corn for...    ...    ...
   Rearrange halfway through cooking.

| Microwave oven in use for 11 minutes | |
| --- | --- |
| Approximate cooking time | Your cooking time |
| 11 minutes | |

*Serving Suggestions.* Serve melted butter separately. Garnish with sprigs of parsley.

*Can be Made in Advance.* Not advisable.

INGREDIENTS

¼ pint (125 ml) water
1 level teaspoon (5 ml) dried yeast
½ teaspoon (2.5 ml) castor sugar
½ oz (15 g) butter
8 oz (250 g) wholemeal flour
1 level teaspoon (5 ml) salt
*Topping*
1 small tin of tomatoes
1 teaspoon (5 ml) mixed herbs
½ teaspoon (2.5 ml) of Season All
Salt and pepper to taste
1 oz (25 g) cheese (Cheddar)
Garnish: anchovies and olives

| Microwave oven in use for 6 minutes |
|---|

METHOD

| | Approximate cooking time | Your cooking time |
|---|---|---|
| 1) Place the water in a jug and heat in the oven for ... ... ... | 30 seconds | |
| 2) Stir into the warm water the yeast and sugar. Leave to stand until the yeast has dissolved – about 5 minutes. | | |
| 3) Rub the butter into the flour and add the salt. Mix in the yeast liquid to form a dough. Turn on to a lightly floured board and knead well. Form into a flattish round shape and place in a greased plate pie dish. | | |
| 4) Cover with cling film and place into the oven to heat for ... ... | 30 seconds | |

5) Remove from the oven leaving the film in position for the first 10 minutes. Leave to stand until approximately doubled in size – 20 minutes. Prepare the topping whilst waiting for the dough to rise.

6) Drain the tomatoes and slice. Mix them with the herbs and season. Grate the cheese.

7) Place the risen dough in the oven to cook for ... ... ...     $3\frac{1}{2}$ minutes

8) Remove and spread the tomato mixture over the dough. Return to the oven to cook for ... ...     1 minute

9) Sprinkle the cheese over the tomato mixture and return to the oven to melt the cheese for ...     30 seconds or until the cheese has melted.

*Serving Suggestions.* Garnish with strips of drained anchovies and olives. Serve hot.

*Can be Made in Advance.* Suitable to refrigerate overnight, or for freezing.

## CHEESY MUSHROOMS Starter

INGREDIENTS
½ lb (250 g) mushrooms
1 oz (25 g) butter
1 oz (25 g) flour
½ pint (250 ml) milk
2 oz (50 g) finely grated cheese
Salt and pepper to taste
Garnish: parsley

*Microwave oven in use for 6¼ minutes*

METHOD

| | Approximate cooking time | Your cooking time |
|---|---|---|
| 1) Peel and slice the mushrooms and arrange in a dish. Cover, cook for ... ... ... ... ... | 3 minutes | |
| 2) Remove from the oven and leave to stand whilst preparing the sauce. | | |
| 3) Place the butter in a jug. Melt the butter for ... ... ... ... | 30 seconds | |
| 4) Stir in the flour and milk. Return to the oven to cook for ... ... Stir every minute. | 3 minutes | |
| 5) Remove from the oven and stir in the cheese. Adjust the seasoning. | | |
| 6) Drain the liquor from the mushrooms. Pour the sauce over the mushrooms. | | |

*Serving Suggestions.* Serve with hot toast. Garnish with parsley.

*Can be Made in Advance.* Sauce could be made earlier and re-heated.

# VEAL À LA MAISON

INGREDIENTS

2 oz (50 g) unsalted butter
8 oz (250 g) onions
6 oz (150 g) mushrooms
1½ lb (750 g) veal
½ teaspoon (2.5 ml) mace
½ teaspoon (2.5 ml) rosemary
2 oz (50 g) flour
One 10 oz (250 g) tin sliced carrots
One 15 oz (approx. 375 ml) tin cream
    of chicken soup
¼ pint (125 ml) dry sherry
Garlic salt
Pepper
Garnish: parsley

*Microwave oven in use
for 19½ minutes*

METHOD

| | Approximate cooking time | Your cooking time |
|---|---|---|
| 1) Put butter into large bowl. Melt the butter for ... ... ... | 1½ minutes | |
| 2) Peel and finely dice onions, slice mushrooms, and cube the veal removing any sinews. Mix these with the butter, cover bowl. Cook for ... ... ... ... Stir the veal about every 3 minutes. | 12 minutes | |
| 3) After 12 minutes sprinkle in the herbs, stir in the flour, add the drained carrots, stir in the soup and sherry. Cover bowl. Cook for ... ... ... ... ... Stir halfway through cooking. | 6 minutes | |
| 4) Remove from microwave oven and allow to stand for 5 minutes. | | |
| 5) Adjust seasoning with garlic salt and pepper. | | |

*Serving Suggestions.* Garnish with parsley and lemon wedges. Serve on a bed of saffron rice with broccoli.

*Can be Made in Advance.* Suitable to refrigerate overnight or for freezing.

## PORK IN WINE

INGREDIENTS

Four 6 oz (150 g each) pork fillets
Oil
1 oz (25 g) unsalted butter
2 oz (50 g) butter
4 oz (100 g) onion
2 oz (50 g) flour
¼ pint (125 ml) red wine
One 15 oz (approx. 375 ml) tin
    tomato soup
1 teaspoon (5 ml) mixed herbs
Garlic salt
Pepper
Garnish: parsley

| Microwave oven in use for 17 minutes |
| --- |

METHOD

| | Approximate cooking time | Your cooking time |
| --- | --- | --- |
| 1) Brush the fillets lightly with oil and arrange them in a flat dish with sides. Dot each with unsalted butter, cover with a lid or cling film. Cook for ... ... ... | 5 minutes | |
| 2) Turn and rearrange the pork fillets as necessary to achieve even cooking. Cover and return to the oven for a further ... ... ... When cooked set aside whilst making the sauce. | 3 minutes | |
| 3) In a large jug or bowl melt the butter for ... ... ... ... | 1½ minutes | |

| | |
|---|---|
| 4) Peel and finely chop the onion and add this to the melted butter. Cover the jug and cook for ... | 1½ minutes |
| 5) Stir in the flour and then the wine, tomato soup and herbs. Place the sauce in the oven and cook for ... | 4 minutes |
| 6) Season to taste with garlic salt and pepper. If a slightly thinner sauce is desired add the juices from the pork fillets. Arrange fillets in dish. Pour over sauce. | |
| 7) Cover the dish and return to the oven to heat through for ... ... | 1½–2 minutes |

*Serving Suggestions.* Garnish with parsley. Serve surrounded by piped potatoes. Serve separately fried cauliflower, apples, peas.

*Can be Made in Advance.* Suitable to refrigerate overnight or for freezing.

INGREDIENTS

One 15 oz (approx. 375 ml) tin sliced peaches

4 gammon steaks approx. 5 oz (125 g) each

½ oz (15 g) cornflour (optional)

Garnish: parsley sprigs and peaches

| | *Microwave oven in use for 8½ minutes* | |
|---|---|---|

METHOD

| | *Approximate cooking time* | *Your cooking time* |
|---|---|---|
| 1) Drain the peaches and place 2 slices of peach on to each gammon and roll up. Secure each with a wooden cocktail stick. | | |
| 2) Arrange the rolled steaks in a shallow dish and cover loosely with cling film. Cook for... ... | 4 minutes | |
| 3) Turn each steak over and pour on the peach syrup. Cover the dish with cling film. Cook for... ... | 1½ minutes | |
| 4) Arrange the remaining peaches over the steaks, cover and heat for ... ... ... ... ... | 1 minute | |
| 5) Leave to stand for 3–5 minutes before serving. | | |
| 6) If a thicker sauce is desired pour off the liquid and make up to ½ pint (250 ml) with water. Put the cornflour in a measuring jug and slowly blend in the liquid. Cook for ... Check and stir every ½ minute to ensure a smooth result. | 2 minutes | |
| 7) Pour the sauce over the steaks or serve separately. | | |

*Serving Suggestions.* Garnish with sprigs of parsley and any remaining peaches. Serve separately sauté potatoes, and corn mixed with peas.

*Can be Made in Advance.* Suitable to refrigerate overnight or for freezing.

# LAMB CHOPS AU NATUREL

**Main Course**

### INGREDIENTS

3 tablespoons (45 ml) oil
3 tablespoons (45 ml) vinegar
1 tablespoon (15 ml) chopped onion
½ teaspoon (2.5 ml) pepper
4 lamb chops approx. 6 oz (150 g) each
Garnish: slices of tomatoes

*Microwave oven in use for 4 minutes*

### METHOD

1) Mix all the ingredients together and pour this over the chops. Leave to stand for at least 15 minutes but longer if possible.

2) Drain the chops and if desired brown them under the grill or in a frying pan. If this is not done it will be necessary to extend the cooking time for a few minutes.

3) Arrange the chops on a plate or a similar dish. Cover loosely with a roasting bag. Cook for ...    ...

4) Remove the chops and leave to stand covered for approximately 3 minutes before serving.

| Approximate cooking time | Your cooking time |
|---|---|
| 4 minutes | |

*Serving Suggestions.* Garnish with slices of tomatoes. Serve with new buttered potatoes tossed in parsley, green beans. Serve mint jelly separately.

*Can be Made in Advance.* Not advisable.

6

INGREDIENTS

1 large onion
1 large 16 oz (500 g) tin drained kidney beans
1 large 16 oz (500 g) tin tomatoes
1 oz (25 g) butter
1 lb (500 g) minced beef
1 level tablespoon (15 ml) chilli powder
½ teaspoon (2.5 ml) cumin
1 clove garlic crushed
1 oz (25 g) flour
1 tablespoon (15 ml) tomato purée
Garnish: parsley and lemon wedges

> Microwave oven in use
> for 12 minutes

METHOD

| | Approximate cooking time | Your cooking time |
|---|---|---|
| 1) Peel and finely chop the onion, drain the beans, roughly chop the tomatoes. | | |
| 2) Place the butter into a large bowl. Melt butter for ... ... ... | 1 minute | |
| 3) Stir in the onions, cover the bowl and return to the oven to cook for ... ... ... ... ... | 3 minutes | |
| 4) Stir in the remaining ingredients, cover the bowl and place in the oven to cook for ... ... ... Stir halfway through cooking. | 8 minutes | |
| 5) Remove from the oven and leave to stand for 3–4 minutes before serving. | | |

*Serving Suggestions.* Serve on a bed of rice. Garnish with parsley and lemon wedges, with a mixed side salad.

*Can be Made in Advance.* Suitable to refrigerate overnight or for freezing.

# COLD SAVOURY MEAT LOAF

## INGREDIENTS

1 oz (25 g) butter
1 large onion
1 lb (500 g) minced beef
2 oz (50 g) white breadcrumbs
1 teaspoon (5 ml) mixed herbs
8 oz (250 g) sausage meat
Garlic salt and pepper to taste
2 eggs
Garnish: sliced tomatoes and lettuce

> *Microwave oven in use
> for 12 minutes*

## METHOD

| | Approximate cooking time | Your cooking time |
|---|---|---|
| 1) Place the butter into a large bowl. Melt for ... ... ... ... | 1 minute | |
| 2) Stir in the peeled and finely diced onion, cover the bowl and return to the oven to cook for ... ... | 3 minutes | |
| 3) Stir in all the other ingredients with the exception of the eggs. Cover the bowl and return to the oven to cook for ... ... ... | 4 minutes | |
| 4) Mix in the eggs and put the mixture into a greased and lined container. Cover the container and cook for ... ... ... ... ... | 4 minutes | |
| 5) Remove from the oven, remove the cover and leave to cool. Turn out when cold. | | |

*Serving Suggestions.* Serve on a bed of lettuce. Garnish with slices of tomatoes. Serve potato salad and coleslaw separately.

*Can be Made in Advance.* Suitable to refrigerate overnight or for freezing.

INGREDIENTS

1 large onion
½ lb (250 g) carrots
½ lb (250 g) tomatoes
¼ lb (125 g) mushrooms
2 oz (50 g) butter
1 teaspoon (5 ml) mixed herbs
½ pint (250 ml) hot water
1 beef stock cube
4 lamb chops (1–1½ lb) (500–750 g)
2 oz (50 g) instant potato (optional)
Salt and pepper to taste

> *Microwave oven in use for 17¼ minutes*

METHOD

| Method | Approximate cooking time | Your cooking time |
|---|---|---|
| 1) If desired, brown the chops under the grill or in a frypan. | | |
| 2) Peel and finely slice the onion and the carrots. Skin the tomatoes and slice. Wash and slice the mushrooms. | | |
| 3) Cut the butter into knobs and place into a large bowl. Melt butter for ...   ...   ...   ... | 1½ minutes | |
| 4) Stir in the onions and carrots. Cover bowl and cook for...   ... | 4 minutes | |
| 5) Stir in the mushrooms, tomatoes and the herbs. Cover and cook for ...   ...   ...   ...   ... | 2 minutes | |
| 6) Stir in the water, stock cube and chops. Cover and cook for   ... Turn the bowl and stir after 5 minutes. | 10 minutes | |
| 7) If a thicker sauce is desired remove the chops and stir in the instant potato. Adjust the seasoning and pour the sauce over the chops. | | |

*Serving Suggestions.* Serve with creamed potatoes.

*Can be Made in Advance.* Suitable to refrigerate overnight or for freezing.

INGREDIENTS

1½ lb (750 g) sirloin steak
1 large onion
8 oz (250 g) diced green and red
   peppers
2 oz (50 g) unsalted butter
2 oz (50 g) flour
½ pint (250 ml) brown ale
½ pint (250 ml) water
1 beef stock cube
2 tablespoons (30 ml) tomato purée
1 teaspoon (5 ml) mixed herbs
Salt and pepper to taste
Garnish: parsley

> Microwave oven in use
> for 14¼ minutes

METHOD

| METHOD | Approximate cooking time | Your cooking time |
|---|---|---|
| 1) Cut the meat into cubes. Peel and finely dice the onion. De-seed and finely dice the pepper. | | |
| 2) Cut the butter into knobs and place into a large bowl. Melt for ... ... ... ... ... | 1½ minutes | |
| 3) Add the meat to the butter and cook for ... ... ... ... Stir halfway through cooking. | 3 minutes | |
| 4) Remove the meat and to the butter mixture add the peppers and the onion. Cook for ... ... ... Stir halfway through cooking. | 4 minutes | |
| 5) Stir in the flour and the remaining ingredients. Cook for ... ... Stir after 3 minutes. Remove from the oven and adjust the seasoning. | 6 minutes | |

*Serving Suggestions.* Garnish with parsley. Serve with potatoes tossed in chopped parsley and a purée of turnips and carrots.

*Can be Made in Advance.* Suitable to refrigerate overnight or for freezing.

## MEAT BALLS IN TOMATO SAUCE

INGREDIENTS

1 lb (500 g) minced beef
1 oz (25 g) white breadcrumbs
1 medium size onion, grated
1 teaspoon (5 ml) mixed herbs
Salt and pepper to taste
1 egg beaten
Flour
*Sauce*
1½ oz (40 g) butter
1 large tin tomato soup with sufficient water to make up to 1½ pints (750 ml)
1 beef stock cube
1½ oz (40 g) flour
Salt and pepper to taste
Garnish: parsley

| Microwave oven in use for 16¼ minutes |
|---|

METHOD

1) Mix together the meat, breadcrumbs, grated onion, herbs, salt and pepper and then combine with the egg. With floured hands form the mixture into eight balls.

2) Arrange in a dish and place in the oven to cook for ...   ...   ... Rearrange and turn over halfway through cooking.

3) Remove from the oven, drain off any juice and set aside.

4) Cut the butter into knobs and place into a jug or bowl. Melt for...

| Approximate cooking time | Your cooking time |
|---|---|
| 8 minutes | |
| 1½ minutes | |

| | | |
|---|---|---|
| 5) Stir in the flour and the tomato soup, water and stock cube. | | |
| 6) Place into the oven to cook for ... Stir halfway through cooking. | 4 minutes | |
| 7) Adjust the seasoning and pour over the meat balls. | | |
| 8) Return to the oven to heat for ... | 3 minutes | |

*Serving Suggestions.* Serve surrounded by piped potatoes. Garnish with parsley. Serve with fried courgettes.

*Can be Made in Advance.* Suitable to refrigerate overnight or for freezing.

## BEEF STROGANOFF

INGREDIENTS
1½ lb (750 g) fillet beef
1 large onion
8 oz (250 g) mushrooms
2 oz (50 g) butter
1 oz (25 g) flour
Scant ¼ pint (125 ml) white wine
Salt and pepper to taste
¼ pint (125 ml) soured cream
Garnish: chopped parsley

> Microwave oven in use
> for 10 minutes

METHOD

| | Approximate cooking time | Your cooking time |
|---|---|---|
| 1) Cut the meat into strips. Peel and finely dice the onion. Peel and slice the mushrooms. | | |
| 2) Cut the butter into knobs and place into a large bowl. Melt for ... | 1½ minutes | |
| 3) Add the beef and return to the oven to cook for ... ... ... Stir halfway through cooking. | 3 minutes | |
| 4) Remove the meat. Put the onions and mushrooms into the bowl. Cook for ... ... ... ... Stir halfway through cooking. | 4 minutes | |
| 5) Remove from oven. Stir in the flour, meat and the wine. | | |
| 6) Return to the oven to cook for ... | 1½ minutes | |
| 7) Adjust the seasoning and stir in the soured cream. | | |

*Serving Suggestions.* Garnish with chopped parsley. Serve with croquette potatoes and a mixed side salad.

*Can be Made in Advance.* Suitable to refrigerate overnight or for freezing, but omit the soured cream and stir in just before serving. As the meat is to be reheated, undercook at the cooking stage.

INGREDIENTS
3 lb (1.5 kilo) prepared chicken
1 oz (25 g) melted unsalted butter
Garnish: watercress

METHOD

1) Tie the chicken with string, cover the wings and ends of the legs with foil, brush with butter and put into a roasting bag. Pierce the bag on either side and tie the end loosely with a piece of string.

2) Place the chicken in a dish, breast side down on an upturned saucer. Cook for ...   ...   ...   ...

3) Turn chicken over. Drain off any juices, and return to the oven. Cook for ...   ...   ...   ...

4) Remove from oven, drain off juices, wrap in foil and leave to stand for 10–15 minutes before carving.

N.B. Allow approximately 8 minutes to the lb when cooking chickens. The chicken will not be browned in the conventional manner therefore if it is to be carved at table it can be browned under a preheated grill if desired.

| Microwave oven in use for 24 minutes | |
|---|---|
| Approximate cooking time | Your cooking time |
| 12 minutes | |
| 12 minutes | |

Serving Suggestions. Serve with sausages, french fries, peas. Garnish with watercress. Serve gravy separately.

Can be Made in Advance. Not advisable unless it is to be served jointed, in which case it may be stored in the refrigerator overnight.

# RABBIT IN CREAMY SAUCE          Main Course

INGREDIENTS

1 medium size onion
1 small green pepper
2 oz (50 g) butter
1 teaspoon (5 ml) rosemary
Salt and pepper to taste
½ pint (250 ml) milk
½ pint (250 ml) chicken stock
4 rabbit joints approx. 1½ lb (750 g)
2 oz (50 g) cornflour
¼ pint (125 ml) white wine (or stock if preferred)
Garnish: watercress

*Microwave oven in use for 23 minutes*

METHOD

1) Peel and finely chop the onion. De-seed and finely chop the pepper.

2) Cut the butter into knobs and place in a large bowl. Melt for   ...

3) Stir in the onion and cover the bowl. Cook for  ...     ...     ...

4) Stir into the onion mixture the rosemary, salt and pepper, milk, stock and the rabbit pieces. Cover the bowl. Cook for   ...     ...
After 6 minutes of the cooking time stir the ingredients and repeat again after 5 minutes.

| Approximate cooking time | Your cooking time |
|---|---|
| 1½ minutes | |
| 2½ minutes | |
| 11 minutes | |

5) Remove the rabbit and set aside whilst preparing the sauce.

6) Blend the cornflour to a smooth paste with the wine and stir into the hot milk and stock. Cook sauce for ... ... ... ...    2 minutes
Stir after one minute.

7) Add the rabbit. Cover the bowl. Cook for ... ... ... ...    6 minutes
Turn the bowl and stir at least once during this time.

8) Adjust the seasoning, and serve.

*Serving Suggestions.* Garnish with watercress. Serve with tomato and potato nests, and buttered baby carrots.

*Can be Made in Advance.* Suitable to refrigerate overnight or for freezing.

# DUCKLING WITH ORANGE SAUCE

**Main Course**

## INGREDIENTS

5–5½ lb (2.5–2.75 kilo) duckling
1 orange

*Sauce:*

Rind of 1 orange and the juice of 3 oranges
½ oz (15 g) cornflour
1 tablespoon (15 ml) honey
Garnish: orange slices, watercress

> *Microwave oven in use for 42 minutes*

## METHOD

1) Wash and clean the duckling. Cut orange into 6 segments and place inside the bird. Secure the wings and the legs with string. Place the duckling in a roasting bag and tie the opening up with string. Pierce the bag.

2) Put the bird, breast side down on an upturned saucer in a shallow dish. Cook for ... ... ...

3) Drain off the juices. Replace in the bag and return to the oven with the breast side up. Cook for ...

4) Remove the bird and wrap in foil whilst making the sauce. However, should a crisper skin be desired, place the bird under a preheated grill for a few minutes after the standing time of about 4 minutes.

| Approximate cooking time | Your cooking time |
|---|---|
| 20 minutes | |
| 20 minutes | |

5) Blend the cornflour with the orange juice, grated rind and honey. Make up to $\frac{1}{2}$ pint (250 ml) with some of the duckling juices.

6) Place all the ingredients into a jug. Cook for ...    ...    ...    ... Stir every 30 seconds.

| | |
|---|---|
| 2 minutes | |

*Serving Suggestions.* Garnish the duck with orange slices and watercress. Pour some of the sauce over the bird and serve the remaining sauce separately. Duchesse potatoes, broccoli.

*Can be Made in Advance.* Not advisable.

INGREDIENTS

1½ oz (40 g) butter
½ cooking apple
1 medium size onion
1½ oz (40 g) flour
2 level teaspoons (30 ml) curry
   powder
One 8 oz (250 g) tin tomatoes
1 oz (25 g) brown sugar
½ pint (250 ml) water
1 chicken stock cube
1 oz (25 g) sultanas
Salt and pepper to taste
Juice ½ lemon
8 oz (250 g) diced cooked chicken
   meat
Garnish: desiccated coconut,
   tomatoes

| | *Microwave oven in use for 13½ minutes* |
|---|---|

METHOD

| | Approximate cooking time | Your cooking time |
|---|---|---|
| 1) Place the butter into a large bowl and melt in the oven for ...    ... | 1½ minutes | |
| 2) Peel and finely dice the apples and the onion. Add these to the melted butter, cover and cook for    ... | 3 minutes | |
| 3) Stir in the flour and the curry powder, cover and return to the oven to cook for ...    ...    ... | 1 minute | |
| 4) Stir in all the remaining ingredients except the chicken. Cover and cook in the oven for    ...    ... Stir occasionally, and turn container round, if necessary. | 5 minutes | |

5) Add the diced chicken. Cover and return to the oven to cook for ...

| | |
|---|---|
| 3 minutes | |

6) Allow to stand for a minute or two before serving.

*Serving Suggestions.* Serve on a bed of rice. Garnish with tomatoes and desiccated coconut. Serve separately sliced tomatoes, mango chutney, cucumber salad.

*Can be Made in Advance.* Suitable to refrigerate overnight or for freezing.

# KIDNEYS IN RED WINE

INGREDIENTS

8 lambs kidneys
½ lb (250 g) mushrooms
1 medium size onion
1 oz (25 g) butter
2 oz (50 g) flour
1 teaspoon (5 ml) oregano
1 small tin tomatoes
¼ pint (125 ml) red wine or stock
Salt and pepper to taste
Garnish: chopped parsley

> *Microwave oven in use for 10 minutes*

METHOD

| | Approximate cooking time | Your cooking time |
|---|---|---|
| 1) Remove the skin from the kidneys, cut in four and remove the white cores. Peel and slice the mushrooms. Peel and finely dice the onion. | | |
| 2) Put butter into bowl. Melt butter for ... ... ... ... ... | 1 minute | |
| 3) Stir kidneys, mushrooms and onions into butter. Cover bowl. Cook for ... ... ... ... Stir mixture halfway through cooking. | 6 minutes | |
| 4) Stir in the flour, oregano, tomatoes and wine. Cover bowl, cook for ... | 3 minutes | |
| 5) Stir and leave to stand for 3 minutes before serving. Adjust the seasoning. | | |

*Serving Suggestions.* Serve on a bed of rice. Garnish with chopped parsley. Serve with broccoli.

*Can be Made in Advance.* Suitable for freezing.

# LIVER IN DUBONNET

INGREDIENTS
1 lb (500 g) calves liver
1 oz (25 g) flour
1 medium size onion
2 oz (50 g) butter
1 small tin tomatoes
¼ pint (125 ml) Dubonnet
1 teaspoon (5 ml) sage
Salt and pepper to taste
Garnish: watercress and bacon rolls

*Microwave oven in use for 13 minutes*

METHOD

| | Approximate cooking time | Your cooking time |
|---|---|---|
| 1) Slice liver and toss in the flour. Peel and finely dice onion. Cut butter into knobs. Melt butter for ... ... ... ... ... | 1 minute | |
| 2) Add onions and cover bowl. Cook for ... ... ... ... | 3 minutes | |
| 3) Stir liver and tomatoes into onions. Cover bowl. Cook for ... ... | 5 minutes | |
| 4) Stir in Dubonnet, sage and seasoning. Cover bowl. Cook for ... | 4 minutes | |

5) Remove from oven, stand for 3–5 minutes before serving. Adjust the seasoning.

*Serving Suggestions.* Serve with rice and mixed vegetables. Garnish with watercress and bacon rolls.

*Can be Made in Advance.* Suitable for freezing.

7

## COLD SALMON WITH CUCUMBER SAUCE

INGREDIENTS
*Cucumber Sauce*
1 cucumber
Pepper to taste
1 level teaspoon (5 ml) salt
2 tablespoons (30 ml) white vinegar
4 salmon steaks, 1 inch (250 mm) thick
Garnish: slices of cucumber

| Microwave oven in use for 6 minutes |
|---|

METHOD

|  | Approximate cooking time | Your cooking time |
|---|---|---|

1) Peel and grate the cucumber. Drain well. Mix together pepper, salt and vinegar, and toss the cucumber in this mixture. Chill for at least 30 minutes. Drain before serving.

2) Loosely wrap the salmon steaks in cling film. Cook for ...    ...   — 6 minutes

3) Should the salmon not be quite cooked set timer for a further minute or two. Gently remove steaks and put aside to cool.

*Serving Suggestions.* Garnish with slices of cucumber. Serve with a mixed side salad and hand cucumber sauce separately.

*Can be Made in Advance.* May be refrigerated overnight.

## COD STEAKS WITH CAPER SAUCE

INGREDIENTS

4 cod steaks 1 lb 10 oz (750 g), 1½ inches (375 mm) thick
Melted unsalted butter or oil
1 oz (25 g) butter
1 oz (25 g) flour
½ pint (250 ml) milk
1 egg yolk
1 tablespoon (15 ml) capers
Salt and pepper to taste
Garnish: capers

> *Microwave oven in use for 11 minutes*

METHOD

| | Approximate cooking time | Your cooking time |
|---|---|---|
| 1) Brush fish with melted butter, sprinkle with pepper and arrange in dish. Cover. Cook for ... ... Remove and leave to stand whilst making sauce. | 7 minutes | |
| 2) Place the butter in a jug. Melt for... | 1 minute | |
| 3) Stir in flour and milk. Cook for ... Stir every minute. | 3 minutes | |
| 4) Beat in egg yolk, stir in capers and season to taste. | | |
| 5) Pour the sauce over the fish. Reheat for 2–3 minutes, if necessary. | | |

*Serving Suggestions.* Garnish with capers. Serve with creamed potatoes and tomatoes.

*Can be Made in Advance.* Suitable for freezing.

## STRAWBERRY CLOUD

### INGREDIENTS

Half a 5 oz (125 g) strawberry jelly

8 oz (250 g) strawberry pie filling

¼ pint (125 ml) cold water

7 fl oz (170 ml) evaporated milk

2 tablespoons (30 ml) brandy (optional)

*Topping:*

1½ oz (40 g) digestive biscuits

½ oz (15 g) demerara sugar

½ oz (15 g) chopped walnuts

Decoration: ¼ pint (125 ml) whipped cream

| Microwave oven in use for 1¼ minutes |
| --- |

### METHOD

1) Refrigerate the evaporated milk overnight.

2) Break the jelly into pieces and place into a 1 pint (500 ml) pyrex jug with the water. Melt for ... After 1 minute stir the jelly. Finally remove, stir and leave to cool.

3) Crush the biscuits and mix with the sugar and nuts.

4) Whisk the milk until thick and then slowly whisk in the cold jelly.

5) Whisk in the pie filling and continue until the mixture thickens. If desired add the brandy.

6) Pour the mixture into individual serving dishes or into a large glass dish.

7) Sprinkle the topping over the strawberry mixture.

| Approximate cooking time | Your cooking time |
| --- | --- |
| 1½ minutes | |

*Serving Suggestions.* Serve cold decorated with whipped cream.

*Can be Made in Advance.* Suitable to refrigerate overnight or for freezing.

# ORANGES IN SYRUP

INGREDIENTS

6 oz (50 g) granulated sugar
6 oz (50 ml) cold water
6 oranges
2 tablespoons (30 ml) brandy or Grand Marnier (optional)
Decoration: fine strips of orange peel

| | |
|---|---|
| *Microwave oven in use for 6 minutes* | |

METHOD

| | *Approximate cooking time* | *Your cooking time* |
|---|---|---|
| 1) Stir the sugar and water together in a bowl. Put into microwave oven uncovered for ... ... Stir after 3 minutes. | 6 minutes | |

2) Peel the oranges with a knife, removing both the peel, pith and pips. Slice the oranges into rounds and arrange in four individual dishes or in one large dish. Reserve some peel for decoration.

3) Mix the brandy with the sugar liquid and pour over the oranges.

4) Place in a refrigerator overnight if possible but this is not absolutely necessary.

*Serving Suggestions.* Serve at room temperature with slivers of peel sprinkled over the oranges.

*Can be Made in Advance.* Suitable to refrigerate overnight or for freezing.

## LEMON SORBET

INGREDIENTS
Grated rind of one lemon
Juice of 2 lemons
1 teaspoon (5 ml) gelatine
2 oz (50 g) sugar
1 pint (500 ml) cold water
2 egg whites
Decoration: sprigs of mint

> *Microwave oven in use*
> *for 7 minutes*

METHOD

1) Place all the ingredients with the exception of the egg whites into a large bowl and lightly cover. Heat for ... ... ... ... Stir halfway through cooking.

2) Allow the mixture to cool and then refrigerate until it is on the point of setting.

3) Whisk the egg whites until stiff and peaky. Beat the egg whites into the cold liquid.

4) Pour the sorbet into a container and freeze.

| Approximate cooking time | Your cooking time |
|---|---|
| 7 minutes | |

*Serving Suggestions.* Remove from freezer approximately 30 minutes before serving. Decorate with sprigs of mint.

*Can be Made in Advance.* Suitable for freezing.

## ORANGE SUMMER

INGREDIENTS

1 pint (500 ml) milk
1 packet orange blancmange powder
2 oz (50 g) castor sugar
1 tin mandarin oranges
Decoration: ¼ pint (125 ml) whipping
  cream

| Microwave oven in use for 4½ minutes | | |

METHOD

| | Approximate cooking time | Your cooking time |
|---|---|---|
| 1) Blend ¼ pint (125 ml) of milk with the sugar and blancmange powder. | | |
| 2) Pour ¾ pint (375 ml) of milk into a large jug. Heat milk for... ... | 3 minutes | |
| 3) Pour the hot milk on to the cold mixture and stir well. Return to the oven. Cook the blancmange for... Stir after 1 minute of the cooking time. | 1½ minutes | |
| 4) Pour the blancmange into four serving dishes and leave to cool. | | |
| 5) Drain the mandarin oranges. Whip the cream. | | |
| 6) Decorate the blancmange with the orange segments and whipped cream. | | |

*Serving Suggestions.* Serve refrigerated, decorated with orange segments and swirls of whipped cream.

*Can be Made in Advance.* Refrigerate overnight.

# CHOCOLATE MOUSSE

INGREDIENTS

8 oz (250 g) plain chocolate
1 oz (25 g) butter
4 egg yolks
1 tablespoon (15 ml) brandy (optional)
1 tablespoon (15 ml) strong black coffee
4 egg whites
Decoration: ¼ pint (125 ml) whipping cream

> *Microwave oven in use for 2 minutes*

METHOD

1) Break chocolate into pieces and place into bowl. Melt for...   ...

2) Beat butter into melted chocolate, and beat in egg yolks one at a time. Stir in brandy and coffee.

3) Whisk egg whites until very stiff. Fold egg whites into the chocolate mixture.

4) Pour into four dishes. Set aside to cool.

| Approximate cooking time | Your cooking time |
|---|---|
| 2 minutes | |

*Serving Suggestions.* Serve from refrigerator decorated with swirls of whipped cream.

*Can be Made in Advance.* Suitable to refrigerate overnight or for freezing.

### INGREDIENTS

½ packet lime jelly
¼ pint (125 ml) water
¼ pint (125 ml) double cream
2 avocado pears
Juice of 1 lemon
Decoration: 1 lemon, ¼ pint (125 ml)
    whipping cream

> *Microwave oven in use
> for 1½ minutes*

### METHOD

1) Break the jelly into pieces and place into a jug with the water.

2) Place in the microwave oven and melt for ... ... ... ...

3) Remove the jelly, stir, and leave until almost set.

4) Whip the cream until it makes soft peaks. Whisk the jelly until light and fluffy.

5) Halve the avocados and remove the flesh. Mash the flesh with the lemon juice.

6) Whip the avocado flesh into the jelly and then fold in the cream.

7) Pour the mixture into the four glass dishes. Chill.

| Approximate cooking time | Your cooking time |
|---|---|
| 1½ minutes | |

*Serving Suggestions.* Serve cold decorated with whipped cream and fine slices of lemon.

*Can be Made in Advance.* Suitable to refrigerate overnight or for freezing.

## CHOCOLATE PEARS

INGREDIENTS

4 firm eating pears
1½ pints (750 ml) boiling water
2 oz (50 g) sugar
8 oz (250 g) plain chocolate
Decoration: ¼ pint (125 ml) whipped
    cream, pieces of angelica

| *Microwave oven in use for 14 minutes* | |
|---|---|
| **Approximate cooking time** | **Your cooking time** |

METHOD

1) Carefully peel the pears leaving the stalk in position. If they will not stand upright cut a piece from the base.

2) Pour the boiling water into a large bowl and add the sugar.

3) Add the pears and cook for ...  **12 minutes**
Check the tenderness of the pears every 2 minutes and remove any which are almost cooked.

4) Leave the pears to drain and cool.

5) Break the chocolate into small pieces and place in a large bowl. Melt the chocolate for ...  ...  **2 minutes**

6) Place each pear in turn into the chocolate and coat well with the melted chocolate, avoiding the steam from the fruit.

7) Stand each pear on a piece of foil until the chocolate has set.

*Serving Suggestions.* Carefully remove the foil from the base of each pear and stand in a serving dish surrounded by whipped cream. Decorate with pieces of angelica.

*Can be Made in Advance.* Suitable to refrigerate overnight or for freezing.

INGREDIENTS

4 oz (100 g) sugar
4 oz (100 g) syrup
4 oz (100 g) butter
4 oz (100 g) plain flour
4 drained rings of tinned pineapple
Oil for greasing
Decoration: $\frac{1}{4}$ pint (125 ml) whipping
   cream, 4 glacé cherries

| | *Microwave oven in use for 6 minutes* | |
| --- | --- | --- |
| | *Approximate cooking time* | *Your cooking time* |

METHOD

1) Put the sugar, syrup, and the butter cut into knobs into a large bowl. Melt the ingredients together for ...   ...   ...   ... Stir after 1 minute. — 2 minutes

2) Remove. Leave to stand for 2–3 minutes before beating in the flour to form a smooth paste.

3) Lightly grease a large flat plate and swirl on to this 2 tablespoons (30 ml) of the mixture. Cook for... — 1 minute

4) Remove and set aside whilst cooking three further rounds.

5) When the mixture is cool enough to handle, form into a ball and place on to a drained slice of pineapple. Place the pineapple slice on to a flat serving plate. Mould the mixture over the slice and leave to set. Continue this procedure with each plate of cooked mixture and pineapple slices.

6) When well set remove from the plates and arrange on a serving dish.

*Serving Suggestions.* Serve cold decorated with a swirl of whipped cream and a glacé cherry.
*Can be Made in Advance.* Refrigerated overnight.

# LEMON SOUFFLÉ

INGREDIENTS

3 eggs
2 lemons
2 tablespoons (30 ml) water
½ oz (12 g) gelatine
4 oz (100 g) sugar
7 fl oz (180 ml) evaporated milk
    (Stored in the refrigerator 24 hours
    before use)
Decoration: 2 oz (50 g) chopped nuts
    ¼ pint (125 ml) double cream

| | |
|---|---|
| *Microwave oven in use for 1½ minutes* | |

METHOD

1) Firmly tie a double band of greaseproof paper round a 5½ in. (14 cm) soufflé dish, so that paper stands 2 inches (5 cm) above rim of dish.

2) Separate the eggs, grate the rind and squeeze the juice from the lemons.

3) Combine the water, gelatine, egg yolks and the sugar in a bowl. Cook for ...  ...  ...  ... Stir and check every ½ minute. Remove from the oven and beat until the mixture is thick.

4) Beat in the lemon juice and rind.

5) Beat the evaporated milk until thick and creamy.

| *Approximate cooking time* | *Your cooking time* |
|---|---|
| 1½ minutes | |

6) Whisk the egg whites until stiff. Beat the cooled yolk mixture and then fold the milk into this.

7) Gently fold the egg whites into the yolk milk mixture.

8) Pour the mixture into a prepared 5½ inch (14 cm) soufflé dish. Place into the refrigerator to set.

9) When set gently remove the supporting collar.

*Serving Suggestions.* Decorate the sides with chopped nuts and the top with whipped cream.

*Can be Made in Advance.* Suitable to refrigerate overnight or for freezing.

## INGREDIENTS

*Yeast Mixture*
6 tablespoons (90 ml) milk
1 oz (25 g) castor sugar
½ oz (12 g) dried yeast
3 oz (75 g) butter
8 oz (250 g) plain flour
2 eggs
*Syrup*
4 oz (100 g) granulated sugar
½ pint (250 ml) water
2 tablespoons (30 ml) rum or if preferred the juice of ½ lemon
*Glaze*
8 oz (250 g) apricot jam
1 tablespoon (15 ml) water
Decoration: whipped cream
tin fruit salad

| Microwave oven in use for 9¼ minutes |
| :---: |

## METHOD

| | Approximate cooking time | Your cooking time |
| --- | --- | --- |
| 1) Place milk in a measuring jug and heat in the oven for ... ... | 15 seconds | |
| 2) Stir in 2 teaspoons (10 ml) of sugar and the dried yeast. Leave to stand for 10–15 minutes. | | |
| 3) Rub the butter into the flour and stir in the remaining sugar. | | |
| 4) Beat in the eggs and the yeast liquid until a smooth mix is formed. | | |
| 5) Lightly knead to a smooth ball on a floured board. | | |
| 6) Form into a round and place this into the base of an oiled savarin mould. Cover with cling film. | | |
| 7) Place into the oven and cook for ... ... ... ... Do not remove the cling film. | 30 seconds | |
| 8) Remove from the oven and leave | | |

to double in size – about 30 minutes.

9) Remove the cling film and place into the oven to cook for ...  3 minutes

10) Remove from the oven and leave to stand for approximately 5 minutes before turning out on to a serving dish.

11) Place the granulated sugar into a jug with the water for the syrup and place into the oven. Dissolve the sugar in the water for ...  3 minutes
Stir at 2 minutes. Remove from the oven and stir in the rum or lemon juice.

12) Slowly spoon the syrup over the well pricked savarin until all the syrup has been absorbed. Leave to stand for one hour or longer.

13) Stir the jam and water together in a jug to make the glaze. Heat in the oven for ...  ...  ...  $2\frac{1}{2}$ minutes
Stir at $1\frac{1}{2}$ minutes.

14) Brush the hot glaze over the whole of the savarin.

*Serving Suggestions.* Serve with the drained fruit salad in centre and decorate with cream.

*Can be Made in Advance.* Suitable to refrigerate overnight or for freezing.

INGREDIENTS
*Base*
2 oz (50 g) butter
1 oz (25 g) demerara sugar
4 crushed digestive biscuits
*Filling*
½ lemon jelly
¼ pint (125 ml) water
Rind and juice of one lemon
¼ pint (125 ml) double cream
8 oz (250 g) cream cheese
Decoration: crystallised lemon slices

> Microwave oven in use
> for 2½ minutes

METHOD

| | Approximate cooking time | Your cooking time |
|---|---|---|
| 1) Cut the butter into knobs and place into bowl. Melt butter for ... | 1 minute | |
| 2) Mix the sugar and crushed biscuits into the butter. Line the base of a 6–7 in. (15 cm) flan case. | | |
| 3) Cut the jelly into pieces and place into a jug with the water, grated lemon rind and juice. Melt for ... Stir after 1 minute. | 1½ minutes | |
| 4) Remove jelly, stir and leave to cool. Beat the cream until stiff. | | |
| 5) Beat the cream cheese until soft and then whisk in the jelly. | | |
| 6) Fold in the whipped cream. Pour into case and chill. | | |

*Serving Suggestions.* Decorate with crystallised lemon slices.

*Can be Made in Advance.* Suitable to refrigerate overnight or for freezing.

# CARAMEL EGG CUSTARD

**INGREDIENTS**
*Custard*
1 pint (500 ml) milk
4 large eggs, lightly beaten
1 oz (25 g) castor sugar
2 drops vanilla essence
*Caramel*
2 tablespoons (30 ml) water
2 oz (50 g) castor sugar
Unsalted butter

| Microwave oven in use for 10 minutes |
|---|

**METHOD**

| | Approximate cooking time | Your cooking time |
|---|---|---|
| 1) Make the caramel by placing the water and sugar in a jug. Cook for ... ... ... ... ... Check every ½ minute as the liquid will change to caramel very quickly. | 2 minutes | |
| 2) Pour the caramel into a 2 pint (1 litre) soufflé dish which has been well buttered with unsalted butter. | | |
| 3) Pour the milk into a large bowl or jug. Heat for ... ... ... | 3 minutes | |
| 4) Pour the warmed milk into the lightly beaten eggs, sugar and essence. Strain the egg mixture on to the caramel. Cover the dish with cling film. Cook for ... ... | 5 minutes | |
| 5) Remove the custard from the oven and take off the cling film. | | |
| 6) Leave to cool. When cold turn the custard out on to a serving dish. | | |

*Serving Suggestions.* Serve chilled or at room temperature.

*Can be Made in Advance.* Suitable to refrigerate overnight.

8

INGREDIENTS
*Pastry*
8 oz (250 g) self-raising flour
1 oz (25 g) fresh white breadcrumbs
4 oz (100 g) shredded suet
4 fl oz (100 ml) water
4 oz (100 g) soft brown sugar
Unsalted butter or oil
*Filling and Sauce*
One 14 oz (450 g) tin cherry pie filling
2 tablespoons (30 ml) brandy (optional)

| Microwave oven in use for 14 minutes |
| :---: |

METHOD

1) Mix all the pastry ingredients together. Grease a 2 or 2½ pint (1–1¼ litres) pudding basin with unsalted butter or oil.

2) Divide the pastry into 5 rounds having the first piece smaller than the fifth round.

3) Fit the smallest round of pastry into the bottom of the basin and cover with 1 tablespoon (15 ml) of pie filling. Continue in this way until all the rounds have been used and layered with the pie filling. Finish with a piece of pastry.

| *Approximate cooking time* | *Your cooking time* |
| --- | --- |
|  |  |

4) Cover basin with a greased plate or loosely with cling film, to allow for rise. Cook for...  ...  ... Turn the basin round halfway through cooking.

5) Remove pudding and leave to stand for 4 minutes before turning out. Put the remaining pie filling in an uncovered jug and heat for...

6) Stir the brandy into the sauce.

7) Loosen the sides of the pudding with a knife and turn out on to a serving dish. Pour the hot sauce over the top.

| | |
|---|---|
| 12 minutes | |
| 2 minutes | |

*Serving Suggestions.* Serve hot. Hand cream or custard separately.

*Can be Made in Advance.* Suitable to refrigerate overnight or for freezing.

# HOT APRICOTS IN YOGHURT

INGREDIENTS

One 15 oz (475 g approx.) tin of
  halved apricots
1 oz (25 g) chopped walnuts
5 oz (125 g) natural yoghurt

METHOD

1) Drain the apricots and place into
   a shallow dish. Cover. Heat for ...

2) Remove the dish and arrange the
   apricots in four small serving
   dishes.

3) Pour the refrigerated yoghurt over
   each and sprinkle the nuts over the
   yoghurt.

| Microwave oven in use for 2 minutes | |
|---|---|
| Approximate cooking time | Your cooking time |
| 2 minutes | |

*Serving Suggestions.* Serve immediately.

*Can be Made in Advance.* Not advisable.

## BANANAS GRAND MARNIER Dessert

INGREDIENTS

1 oz (25 g) unsalted butter
2 oz (50 g) demerara sugar
Juice of 2 oranges
4 bananas
Juice of 1 lemon
4 tablespoons (60 ml) Grand Marnier

| | Microwave oven in use for 5 minutes |
|---|---|

METHOD

| | Approximate cooking time | Your cooking time |
|---|---|---|
| 1) Cut the butter into knobs and melt in a basin for ... ... | 30 seconds | |
| 2) Stir in the sugar and orange juice. Heat for ... ... ... ... Remove after 2 minutes if desired. | 2½ minutes | |
| 3) Peel and slice the bananas, toss in lemon juice. Arrange on dish. Heat for ... ... ... ... | 2 minutes | |
| 4) Pour the hot sauce over the bananas. | | |

*Serving Suggestions.* Serve hot. Hand single cream separately.

*Can be Made in Advance.* Not advisable.

INGREDIENTS

6 oz (150 g) golden syrup
3 oz (75 g) butter
4 oz (100 g) soft brown sugar
¼ pint (125 ml) strong black coffee
½ lb (250 g) plain flour
1 small egg
1 level teaspoon (5 ml) baking powder
*Custard*
½ pint (250 ml) milk
1 tablespoon (15 ml) custard powder
1 tablespoon (15 ml) sugar
Decoration: chopped nuts and
    cherries

METHOD

| | *Microwave oven in use for 9¼ minutes* |

| | Approximate cooking time | Your cooking time |
|---|---|---|
| 1) Place syrup, butter cut into knobs, and sugar into bowl. Melt for ... Stir and leave to stand to cool slightly. | 1½ minutes | |
| 2) Beat remaining ingredients into syrup mixture until smooth and pour into a large greased soufflé dish and place into oven. Cook for... ... ... ... ... After 3 minutes turn dish around in the oven. | 5 minutes | |
| 3) Remove from oven, leave to stand. | | |
| 4) Blend the custard ingredients together in a jug. Cook for ... Stir every minute. | 3 minutes | |
| 5) Pour custard over pudding. | | |

*Serving Suggestions.* Serve hot, decorated with chopped nuts and cherries.

*Can be Made in Advance.* Suitable to refrigerate overnight or for freezing.

INGREDIENTS

2 oz (50 g) soft margarine
2 oz (50 g) castor sugar
2 oz (50 g) self-raising flour
1 egg
2 tablespoons (30 ml) blackcurrant pie filling
Decoration: ¼ pint (125 ml) whipped cream

| Microwave oven in use for 6 minutes |
| --- |

METHOD

1) Beat all the ingredients together except the pie filling.

2) Spread the pie filling over the bottom of a greased plate pie dish.

3) Spread the sponge mixture over the pie filling. Cover. Cook for ... Turn round halfway through cooking.

4) Remove from oven. Stand for 3 minutes before turning out.

| Approximate cooking time | Your cooking time |
| --- | --- |
| 6 minutes | |

*Serving Suggestions.* Serve hot or cold with whipped cream.

*Can be Made in Advance.* Suitable to refrigerate overnight or for freezing.

INGREDIENTS
*Pastry*
½ oz (12 g) butter
4 tablespoons (60 ml) water
2 eggs
1 level teaspoon (5 ml) salt
8 oz (250 g) plain flour
*Filling*
4 oz (100 g) mixed dried fruit
1 oz (25 g) butter
2 oz (50 g) soft brown sugar
1 teaspoon (5 ml) mixed spice
¾ lb (375 g) eating apples
Grated rind and juice of 1 lemon
Water for sealing edges
Decoration: ½ oz (15 g) melted butter
   sifted icing sugar

| Microwave oven in use for 8 minutes |
| --- |

METHOD

| | Approximate cooking time | Your cooking time |
| --- | --- | --- |
| 1) To make the pastry, place the butter and the water in a bowl. Melt for ... ... ... ... | 1 minute | |
| 2) Beat the eggs, salt and the flour together in the water, when well mixed cover the pastry and leave to stand for at least 1 hour. | | |
| 3) Place the 1 oz (25 g) butter into a bowl. Melt for ... ... ... | 1 minute | |
| 4) Remove and add sugar, mixed fruit, spice, juice and rind of the lemon and the peeled finely sliced apples. | | |

5) Roll out the pastry to a 14 inch (35 cm) square and cover the whole surface with the fruit mixture leaving the edges free of fruit. Roll up.

6) Pull the two ends round to meet each other in a circle. Seal the two together. Place on a plate. Cook for ...  ...  ...  ...  ... 6 minutes After 4 minutes turn the ring round and brush with ½ oz (15 g) melted butter. Continue cooking.

7) Remove from the oven and leave to stand for a minute or two before sifting over the surface with icing sugar.

*Serving Suggestions.* Serve hot with hot custard sauce.

*Can be Made in Advance.* Suitable for freezing.

INGREDIENTS

3 oz (75 g) butter
4 oz (100 g) treacle
2 oz (50 g) syrup
2 oz (50 g) brown sugar
4 oz (100 g) wholemeal flour
4 oz (100 g) plain flour
A pinch salt
1 level teaspoon (5 ml) bicarbonate soda
1 rounded teaspoon (5 ml) cinnamon
1 rounded teaspoon (5 ml) ginger
1 egg
One 13 oz (425 g) tin apple pie filling
Decoration: whipped cream or custard sauce

> *Microwave oven in use for 7½ minutes*

METHOD

1) Cut the butter into knobs and place into a measuring jug with the treacle, syrup and the sugar. Melt for ...   ...   ...   ...

2) Mix together the flours, salt, bicarbonate soda, cinnamon and ginger. Beat in the melted syrups and the egg to make a smooth batter.

3) Spread the apple pie filling over the base of a greased 9 inch (22 cm) flan dish.

| Approximate cooking time | Your cooking time |
|---|---|
| 1½ minutes | |

| | | |
|---|---|---|
| 4) Evenly pour and spread the ginger mixture over the apples. Cook for ... ... ... ... ... Turn the dish round after 2 and 4 minutes. | 5 minutes | |
| 5) Remove from the oven and leave to stand for 5 minutes before turning out on to a serving dish or plate. | | |
| 6) Return to the oven to heat for ... | 1 minute | |

*Serving Suggestions.* Serve hot with custard sauce or cold decorated with swirls of cream.

*Can be Made in Advance.* Suitable to refrigerate overnight or for freezing.

INGREDIENTS

6 oz (150 g) stale Madeira cake
2 oz (50 g) demerara sugar
1 lb (500 g) apples
2 oz (50 g) butter

| *Microwave oven in use for 5 minutes* | |
|---|---|
| *Approximate cooking time* | *Your cooking time* |

METHOD

1) Crumb the cake and mix with the sugar. Peel, core and thinly slice the apples.

2) In a straight-sided dish layer the apples and cake, finishing with cake crumbs.

3) Melt the butter in a bowl for ... then pour this over the cake crumbs. — **1 minute**

4) Place the apple mixture into oven to cook for ... ... ...
Turn the dish round halfway through cooking. — **4 minutes**

5) Leave to stand for 2 minutes before serving.

*Serving Suggestions.* Serve hot with cream or custard sauce.

*Can be Made in Advance.* Suitable to refrigerate overnight or for freezing.

# Index to Recipes

## STARTERS

## MAIN COURSES

| Meat Balls in Tomato Sauce | 16½ minutes | 86 |
| Beef Stroganoff | 10 minutes | 88 |

*Poultry*

| Succulent Chicken Roast | 24 minutes | 89 |
| Rabbit in Creamy Sauce | 23 minutes | 90 |
| Duckling with Orange Sauce | 42 minutes | 92 |
| Easy Chicken Curry | 13½ minutes | 94 |

*Offal*

| Kidneys in Red Wine | 10 minutes | 96 |
| Liver in Dubonnet | 13 minutes | 97 |

*Fish*

| Cold Salmon with Cucumber Sauce | 6 minutes | 98 |
| Cod Steaks with Caper Sauce | 11 minutes | 99 |

## DESSERTS AND PUDDINGS

| | *Microwave Oven in Use For* | *Page No.* |
|---|---|---|
| *Cold* | | |
| Strawberry Cloud | 1½ minutes | 100 |
| Oranges in Syrup | 6 minutes | 101 |
| Lemon Sorbet | 7 minutes | 102 |
| Orange Summer | 4½ minutes | 103 |
| Chocolate Mousse | 2 minutes | 104 |
| Tangy Avocado | 1½ minutes | 105 |
| Chocolate Pears | 14 minutes | 106 |
| Pineapple Chew | 6 minutes | 107 |
| Lemon Soufflé | 1½ minutes | 108 |
| Simple Savarin | 9¼ minutes | 110 |
| Cheesecake | 2½ minutes | 112 |
| | | |
| *Hot or Cold* | | |
| Caramel Egg Custard | 10 minutes | 113 |
| Cherry Charmer | 14 minutes | 114 |
| Hot Apricots in Yoghurt | 2 minutes | 116 |
| Bananas Grand Marnier | 5 minutes | 117 |
| Moist Coffee Pudding | 9½ minutes | 118 |
| Blackcurrant Pudding | 6 minutes | 119 |
| Strudel Ring | 8 minutes | 120 |
| Apple Ginger Pudding | 7½ minutes | 122 |
| Hot Apple Surprise | 5 minutes | 124 |

# General Index